DK EYEWITNESS

P9-DOH-400

TOP **10**
BEIJING

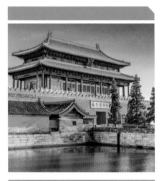

Top 10 Beijing Highlights

The Top 10 of Everything

CONTENTS

Beijing Area by Area

Streetsmart

Within each Top 10 list in this book, no hierarchy of quality or popularity is implied. All 10 are, in the editor's opinion, of roughly equal merit.

Throughout this book, floors are referred to in accordance with American usage; i.e., the "first floor" is at ground level.

Title page, front cover and spine *Colorful boats by the elegant Seventeen-Arch Bridge on Kunming Lake*
Back cover, clockwise from top left *Steamed dumplings; the iconic Great Wall of China at Jinshanling; CCTV Building against the skyline of Central Business District; boats on Kunming Lake at Summer Palace; the impressive Temple of Heaven*

The information in this DK Eyewitness Top 10 Travel Guide is checked regularly. Every effort has been made to ensure that this book is as up-to-date as possible at the time of going to press. Some details, however, such as telephone numbers, opening hours, prices, gallery hanging arrangements and travel information, are liable to change. The publishers cannot accept responsibility for any consequences arising from the use of this book, nor for any material on third party websites, and cannot guarantee that any website address in this book will be a suitable source of travel information. We value the views and suggestions of our readers very highly. Please write to: Publisher, DK Eyewitness Travel Guides, Dorling Kindersley, 80 Strand, London WC2R 0RL, Great Britain, or email travelguides@dk.com

Welcome to
Beijing

From ornate temples and palaces to hip cafés and bars, Beijing's attractions make it a great place to explore. In just over three decades, China's capital has transformed itself from a socialist monolith to a cosmopolitan metropolis, with all the arts, culture, entertainment and glamor that entails. With Eyewitness Top 10 Beijing, it is yours to explore.

Less than 20 years ago, the residents of downtown Beijing were cycling around in their pyjamas, and mules pulling carts of bricks through the streets were a common sight. But over the last decade, the city has experienced an incredible rate of growth. Today, Beijing is dotted with Olympic sites such as the **Bird's Nest** and the **Water Cube**, state-of-the-art venues including the **National Center for the Performing Arts,** and edgy art districts such as **798** and **Caochangdi**, while Sanlitun is filled with chic boutiques.

Yet amid this cosmopolitan city, lovers of antiquities still have plenty to see. The **Forbidden City** anchors the capital, and the **Summer Palace** offers respite from city noise. The conical **Temple of Heaven** graces countless guidebooks, and there are houses of worship on almost every corner – from Taoist (**White Cloud Temple**) to Buddhist (**Lama** and **Fayuan**) and Confucian to Catholic. However, the city's real charm lies in its *hutongs* – 800-year-old warrens that wind through the center – and a walk around **Hou Hai** lake, with its historical courtyard houses, offers a further glimpse of everyday life in Beijing.

Whether you're coming for a weekend or a week, our Top 10 guide brings together the best of everything that Beijing has to offer, from temple fairs to traditional crafts and tea. The guide has useful tips throughout, from seeking out what's free to avoiding the crowds, plus eight easy-to-follow itineraries, designed to tie together a clutch of sights in a short space of time. Add inspiring photography and detailed maps, and you've got the essential pocket-sized travel companion. **Enjoy the book, and enjoy Beijing.**

Clockwise from top: **Great Wall of China, Temple of Heaven, the Forbidden City, Beijing's financial district, painting at the Ming Tombs, the National Stadium, Chinese lanterns**

Exploring Beijing

Beijing combines ancient history with accelerated progress, but information can be sketchy and transportation difficult, even for Chinese speakers. These two itineraries include the city's highlights and offer advice on how to make the most of your time.

Bei Hai Park is a former imperial garden. Its lake is popular for boating.

Two Days in Beijing

Day ❶

MORNING

Do some morning tai chi with the locals at the **Temple of Heaven** (see pp16–17), then browse the art stores on **Liulichang** (see p78). Stop for roast duck at **Deyuan** (see p79), then head into **Tian'an Men Square** (see pp18–19) and the **Forbidden City** (see pp12–15).

AFTERNOON

Leave by the north gate and walk to **Bei Hai Park** (see pp24–5), then over to the **Drum and Bell Towers** (see p26) for a rickshaw ride around the *hutongs* (traditional lanes). Enjoy a Yunnan dinner at **Dali Courtyard** (see p85), then grab a sundowner in **Hou Hai** (see pp26–7).

Day ❷

MORNING

Hire a car for a trip to the **Great Wall** (see pp34–5), and make your way to Mutianyu. After hiking, grab some country-style lunch at a local spot.

AFTERNOON

Visit the **Summer Palace** (see pp28–9). Relax in the Garden of Virtue and Harmony, or go boating on Kunming Lake. End the day with dinner on **Gui Jie** or Ghost Street (see p90).

Four Days in Beijing

Day ❶

MORNING

Start off with the **Forbidden City** (see pp12–15), then wander through **Tian'an Men Square** (see pp18–19). For lunch, head south into the *hutongs* to find **The Southern Fish** (see p79).

AFTERNOON

Visit the **Temple of Heaven** (see pp16–17), then stroll over to **Dazhalan** (see p75) for window shopping, and tasting authentic Chinese tea at **Alice's Tea House** (see p79). Circle back to Qian Men to try Beijing's famous dish in an authentic setting at **Liqun Roast Duck Restaurant** (see p79).

Day ❷

MORNING

Join the locals in **Bei Hai Park** (see pp24–5) for some morning tai chi

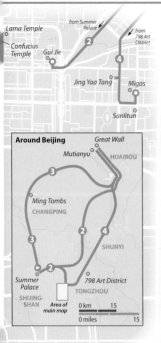

Key
— Two-day itinerary
— Four-day itinerary

and water calligraphy, then wander over toward the **Drum and Bell Towers** in Hou Hai (see pp26–7). Get lost in the *hutongs* and stop at **Mr Shi's Dumplings** (see p57) for lunch.
AFTERNOON
Continue down leafy Guozijian Street. Check out the traditional craft shops and **Confucius Temple** (see p82) before heading to the **Lama Temple** (see pp20–21). Dine on excellent

The Hall of Prayer for Good Harvests can be found at **The Temple of Heaven**.

The Great Wall at Mutianyu dates from the 14th century.

Yunnan food on the terrace at **Yun Er** (see p85), then wander down bustling Nanluoguxiang for some craft beer at the **Great Leap Brewery** (see p84).

Day ❸
MORNING
Get an early start and hire a private car to take you to the **Summer Palace** (see pp28–9). Stop at the **Ming Tombs** (see pp32–3), then go on to the **Great Wall** (see pp34–5). Enjoy a late countryside lunch at Mutianyu.
AFTERNOON
Hike to your heart's content, then sleep on a *kang* (traditional bed) in a farmer's house after a rustic dinner.

Day ❹
MORNING
Leave after breakfast and head back to the city, stopping at the **798 Art District** (see pp30–31).
AFTERNOON
Grab lunch at **AT Café** (see p31), and check out some of the galleries that have made Chinese art famous. Head back downtown to Sanlitun for authentic Chinese cuisine at **Jing Yaa Tang** (see p93), then take a wander over to **Migas** (see p93) for alfresco after-dinner drinks.

Top 10 Beijing Highlights

Colorful pavilion atop the
Forbidden City's North Gate

Beijing Highlights

At the heart of Beijing is tradition, symbolized by the Forbidden City, home to successive imperial dynasties for five centuries. Nearby, Tian'an Men Square is the China of recent times, of socialism and Mao. Beijing is also a city on the move, as a spirit of change makes it the most 21st century of capitals.

Forbidden City

So called because at one time only members of the imperial court were allowed inside, this is one of the largest and greatest palace complexes ever built (see pp12–15).

Temple of Heaven

Originally the venue for annual winter solstice sacrifices, which were performed by successive emperors to ensure ample harvests, the temple remains Beijing's most recognizable icon (see pp16–17).

Tian'an Men Square

The world's largest public square is not pretty, but it is surrounded by august cultural and political institutions, and it is also the final resting place of Chairman Mao Zedong (see pp18–19).

Lama Temple

The largest and most spectacular of the city's temples is a working lamasery, home to monks from Mongolia and Tibet (see pp20–21).

Bei Hai Park

The most beautiful of Beijing's many city parks is laid out around a central lake, first dug out in the 12th century, with the excavated earth used to create a central island. The famed Kublai Khan ruled his empire from a palace here (see pp24–5).

6 Hou Hai
By day visitors take rickshaw tours around the back lanes for a glimpse of fast-disappearing old Beijing; by night, attention shifts to the area's lakeside bars and restaurants (see pp26–7).

Around Beijing

7 Summer Palace
Beijing summers are unbearably hot, so the imperial court would exchange the Forbidden City for this semi-rural retreat, with its ornate pavilions and gardens, ranged around Kunming Lake (see pp28–9).

8 798 Art District
When former electronic components factory 798 became a venue for contemporary art, it kick-started a local trend for converting industrial spaces into galleries and chic bars (see pp30–31).

9 Ming Tombs
Thirty miles (45 km) northwest of Beijing is the vast burial site of 13 of China's 16 Ming emperors. The most impressive sight here is the Sacred Way, with its 12 pairs of stone guardians (see pp32–3).

10 Great Wall of China
"Great" is something of an understatement; the Wall is nothing less than spectacular. Clamber up the perilously sloping carriageways to one of the highest watchtowers on the wall – the experience is breathtaking (see pp34–5).

🔟 ⭐ Forbidden City

Officially known as the Palace Museum, this magnificent complex is a grand monument to the 24 emperors who ruled from its halls over a period of almost 500 years. The symbolic center of the Chinese universe, the palace was the exclusive domain of the imperial court from its completion in 1420 until the last of the emperors was forced to abdicate at the beginning of the 20th century. The modern world intruded in 1949, when the public were finally admitted through the palace gates. A limit of 80,000 visitors per day remains in force.

Meridian Gate ①
Known in Chinese as the *Wu Men*, this gate is the traditional entrance to the palaces. From the balcony **(right)** the emperor would review his armies and perform ceremonies marking the start of the new lunar year.

② Hall of Supreme Harmony
Raised on a triple tier of marble terraces, this largest of halls houses a sandalwood throne **(left)**, used in the coronations of 24 emperors.

③ Inner Court
The Inner Court is more intimate than the formal Outer Court, because this is where the emperor and empress lived, close to the emperor's concubines.

④ Imperial Garden
The emperor Qianlong wrote, "Every ruler [...] must have a garden in which he can stroll, and relax his heart." This formal garden, the oldest in the Forbidden City, has two beautiful pavilions **(below)**.

NEED TO KNOW

MAP L3 ■ North of Tian'an Men Square ■ 8500 7422 ■ Subway: Tian'an Men West or Tian'an Men East ■ en.dpm.org.cn

Open Apr–Oct: 8:30am–5pm Tue–Sun; Nov–Mar: 8:30am–4:30pm Tue–Sun

Adm Apr–Oct ¥60; Nov–Mar ¥40 (buy tickets online in advance); there are additional charges of ¥10 for certain halls; audio guides are available for ¥40 (plus ¥100 deposit)

■ There are snack kiosks near the ticket office, and a restaurant inside.

■ Enter through the Meridian Gate only; other gates are for exit.

7 Hall of Preserving Harmony

The most spectacular aspect of this hall **(left)** is the great carved ramp on the north side, sculpted with dragons and clouds, and made from a single piece of marble weighing more than 200 tons.

Forbidden City

10 Gate of Supreme Harmony

The fourth and final great gate gives access to the Outer Court, the heart of the Forbidden City. The gate is guarded by two large bronze lions, classic imperial symbols of power and dignity.

5 Eastern Palaces

East of the Inner Court are smaller halls. This is where the emperor's harem once lived.

6 Western Palaces

It took a decade to restore the Western Palaces, with six now open to the public. These include the Palace of Gathered Elegance and the Palace of Eternal Spring, both associated with the Empress Dowager Cixi *(see p29)*.

8 Gate of Heavenly Purity

The oldest hall of all is the boundary between the Outer Court (official) and Inner Court (private).

9 Golden Water

Five bridges span the Golden Water **(below)**, which flows from west to east in a course designed to resemble the jade belt worn by the court officials.

⓾ Forbidden City Collections

① Ceramics

Several halls around the Inner Court display tomb figurines from the Sui (581–618) and Tang (618–906) dynasties. Statues range from six inches to three feet (15 cm to 1 m) in height, and depict overweight court ladies, Buddhas on elephants, and floppy-humped camels. A film offers some background on the pottery finds.

Delicately decorated ceramic vase

② Scientific Instruments

Enlightened Qing emperor Kangxi (1654–1722) appointed Europeans as court officials, and instructed his imperial workshops to re-create Western scientific instruments. These included astronomical tools, calculators, sundials, and a table with measurements and scientific notations. The instruments are part of the Imperial Treasures of the Ming and Qing dynasties exhibit in the Palace of Earthly Tranquility.

③ Jade

The Hall of Spiritual Cultivation was once where dowager empresses went to die; it now exhibits jade artifacts. Pieces range from simple cups and ladles to enormous and intricate sculptures of Buddhas in traditional settings. The Chinese considered working this hard stone to be a metaphor for character development and the pursuit of perfection.

④ Jewelry

Three of the six "jewelry" halls lie in the Palace of Tranquil Longevity (head north for rooms four through six), including the only hall to display traditional jewelry rather than agate cups or jade sculpture. Hall number three has thick jade rings, lapis lazuli court beads, elaborate headdresses made of gold filigree phoenixes, and even jadeite Christian rosary beads.

⑤ Beijing Opera

The Belvedere of Pleasant Sounds sports a three-story stage able to accommodate 1,000 actors. It was once rigged with trapdoors and pulleys to create dramatic entrances for supernatural characters. The exhibits include a behind-the-scenes model stage, as well as costumes, instruments, scripts, and cast lists. Screens show reconstructions of old court performances.

Dramatic scene unfolding on stage during a Beijing Opera performance

6 Musical Instruments

In true imperial fashion, the more lavish the musical entertainment, the more glory it reflected on the emperor. Court musicians used gongs of all sizes and *guqins* (zithers), wooden flutes, and heavy bronze bells adorned with dragons, as well as the unusual *sheng*, a Sherlock Holmes-style pipe with reeds of different lengths sprouting from the top. The collection is displayed in the Tower of Enhanced Righteousness, on the west side of the Outer Court.

Pagoda-topped four-sided clock

embroidered red silk decorated with ornate Chinese mythological symbols.

9 Clocks and Watches

Arguably the finest of all the palace treasures, the collection of clocks and watches fills the Hall for Ancestral Worship in the southeastern corner of the eastern Inner Court. The creativity involved in some of the pieces, which are primarily of European origin, is astonishing. One particularly inventive model has an automaton clad in a European dress, frantically writing eight Chinese characters on a scroll, which is being unrolled by two other mechanical figures.

10 Empress Cixi

The Xianfu Pavilion is a memorial to the Empress Cixi's devious rise to power *(see p29)*, as well as to the great lady's imperial extravagances, which nearly crippled her country. Clothes, jewelry, embroidered socks, imported perfume, jade and ivory chopsticks, and pictures of clothes and food form the bulk of the exhibits. There are also examples of the empress's calligraphic skills in the form of painted wall hangings.

Empress Cixi's display, Xianfu Pavilion

Bells in the instrument collection

7 Stone Drums

The Hall of Spiritual Cultivation holds the palace's collection of stone drums. These are enormous tom-tom shaped rocks that bear China's earliest stone inscriptions, dating back to 374 BC. These ideographic carvings, arranged in four-character poems, commemorate the glorious pastureland and successful animal husbandry that were made possible under the Emperor Xiangong's benevolent rule.

8 Daily Life of the Concubines

Every three years, court officials would select girls between the ages of 13 and 17 to join the eight ranks of imperial concubines. The Yonghe Pavilion exhibits clothing, games, herbal medicine, and a food distribution chart relating to the young imperial consorts, as well as the "wedding night bed," which is covered in a richly

🔟 ⭐ Temple of Heaven (Tian Tan)

As the Son of Heaven, the emperor could intercede with the gods on behalf of his people. It was here that he would pray at the winter solstice for a good harvest. Off-limits to the common people during the Ming and Qing dynasties, the complex is now open to the public and attracts thousands of visitors daily, including many locals who come to enjoy the huge park in which the temple is set.

① Hall of Prayer for Good Harvests
Built in 1420, then rebuilt in 1889, this circular tower, with a conical roof of blue tiles and a gold finial, is the most beautiful building in Beijing. One of the most striking facts about it is that it was constructed without the use of a single nail.

② Painted Caisson Ceiling
The circular ceiling of the Hall of Prayer for Good Harvests has a gilded dragon and phoenix at its center **(below)**. The wood for the four central columns was imported from Oregon, as at the time China had no trees tall enough.

③ Temple of Heaven Park
Today, locals, inured to both the splendor of the buildings and the crowds of tourists, use the vast grounds to practice tai chi and to exercise.

④ Imperial Vault of Heaven
A circular hall made of wood and capped by a conical roof, the Imperial Vault **(above)** once held the wooden spirit tablets that were used in the ceremonies that took place on the nearby Round Altar.

⑤ Round Altar
The altar is formed of marble slabs laid out in nine concentric circles with each gray circle containing a multiple of nine pieces. The center of the altar represents the center of the world and it is where the emperor carried out sacrifices.

6 Echo Stones

There are three rectangular stones at the foot of the staircase leading up to the Imperial Vault: stand on the first and clap to hear one echo; stand on the second stone and clap once for two echoes; clap once on the third for three echoes.

Temple of Heaven (Tian Tan)

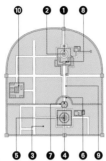

TIAN TAN

The Hall of Prayer for Good Harvests, or Qinian Dian, which is the iconic structure at the heart of the complex, is often incorrectly called the Temple of Heaven. There is, in fact, no single temple building and the name, which in Chinese is Tian Tan – a more literal translation of which is Altar of Heaven – refers to the whole complex.

Marble Platform 8

The Hall of Prayer for Good Harvests sits atop three tiers of marble that form a circle 300 ft (90 m) in diameter (right). The balusters on the upper tier are decorated with carvings of dragons that signify the imperial nature of the structure.

9 Red Step Bridge

A raised walkway of marble and stone that runs along the north-south axis of the complex, the Red Step Bridge (below) connects the Hall of Prayer for Good Harvests with the Round Altar.

7 Echo Wall

The Imperial Vault is enclosed by the circular Echo Wall, which has the same sonic effects found in some European cathedrals, where even a whisper travels round to a listener on the other side.

NEED TO KNOW

MAP F6 ■ Tian Tan Dong Lu (East Gate), Chongwen ■ 6702 2483 ■ Subway: Tian Tan Dong Men ■ en.tiantanpark.com

Park: open 6am–10pm daily; adm ¥15

■ *Temple:* open 8am–5:30pm daily (Jul–Oct: to 6pm; Nov–Feb: to 5pm);

adm ¥35, audio guides ¥40, plus deposit of ¥100

■ There are snack kiosks in the park grounds.

■ Just as fascinating as exploring the temple is observing the many Chinese who come to the park to dance, exercise, sing opera, and fly kites.

10 Hall of Abstinence

A red-walled compound surrounded by a moat spanned by bridges, this hall resembles a mini Forbidden City. This is where the emperor would spend the last 24 hours of his three-day fast prior to partaking in the Temple of Heaven ceremonies.

TOP10 ⭐ Tian'an Men Square

Tian'an Men Guangchang (Square of the Gate of Heavenly Peace) is not the world's most attractive public plaza. It also has unfortunate associations with death, in the shape of Mao's Mausoleum and in the memories of the bloody climax of 1989's pro-democracy rallies. However, it is central to modern life in Beijing, surrounded by major national institutions, and filled daily with visitors and kite flyers.

1 National Museum of China

The largest museum in China **(below)** houses several exhibitions which showcase the history, art and archaeological arti-facts of the Chinese civilization. It is also the second most-visited museum in the world.

4 Tian'an Men

On October 1, 1949, Mao proclaimed the founding of the People's Republic of China from this massive Ming-dynasty gate **(right)**, where his huge portrait is still prominently displayed. The way to the Forbidden City is through here.

6 Railway Museum

Built by the British in 1906, China's first ever passenger train station now houses a Railway Museum. Perfect for train enthusiasts, old photos, model trains, and a full-sized replica of a modern high-speed train driver's cabin are on display.

2 Great Hall of the People

A monolithic structure dominating the western side of the square, the Great Hall is the seat of the Chinese legislature. The vast auditorium and banqueting halls are open for part of every day except when the People's Congress is in session.

5 Arrow Tower

Along with the Qian Men, the Arrow Gate formed part of a great double gate. The walls that once flanked the gate were eventually demolished in the 20th century.

Qian Men 3

Also known as Zhengyang Men ("Sun-facing Gate"), the "Front Gate" **(right)** was built during the Ming dynasty. It was the largest of the nine gates of the inner city wall. It now houses a city history museum.

7 National Flag
The Chinese flag flies at the northern end of Tian'an Men Square. People's Liberation Army (PLA) soldiers raise the flag each day at dawn and lower it back down again as the sun begins to set over the city.

9 Bicycles
While there are allegedly 10 million bikes registered in Beijing, every day as many as 1,300 new cars are added to the city's congested roads. Smog levels in the city are a serious problem.

CITY WALLS

It was during the Ming era (1368–1644) that the walls took on their recognizable shape of an outer wall with seven gates, and an inner wall with nine gates. Rather tragically, almost all was demolished in the 1950s and 1960s, although a small portion still stands south of Beijing Station. Today the gates are remembered in the names of the subway stations situated on the Second Ring Road.

Tian'an Men Square

8 Mao's Mausoleum
In an imposing hall at the center of Tian'an Men Square lies the embalmed body of Mao Zedong, who died in 1976. Encased in a crystal casket and draped in a red flag, the founding father of Communist China is raised from his refrigerated chamber for daily public viewings.

NEED TO KNOW

MAP L5 ■ Subway: Tian'an Men West, Tian'an Men East, or Qian Men

National Museum of China: 6511 6400; open 9am–5pm Tue–Sun (Jul & Aug: 7–11am Tue–Sun); free with valid ID; en.chnmuseum.cn

Mao's Mausoleum: 6513 2277; open 8am–noon Tue–Sun; free with valid ID; carrying handbags, backpacks, cameras, food and drinks inside, and wearing vests or sandals is prohibited

Qian Men: 6522 9384; open 9am–4.30pm Tue–Sun; adm ¥20

Railway Museum: 6705 1638; open 9am–5pm Tue–Sun; adm ¥20

Tian'an Men: 6524 3322; open 8:30am–4:30pm daily; adm ¥15

■ Entry involves security checks, so schedule plenty of time for lines.

10 Monument to the Heroes
Erected in 1958, the granite monument **(below)** is decorated with bas-reliefs of episodes from the nation's revolutionary history and calligraphy from Communist veterans Mao Zedong and Zhou Enlai.

ᵀᴼᴾ10 ⭐ Lama Temple (Yonghe Gong)

Beijing's most spectacular place of worship is also the most famous Buddhist temple outside of Tibet. It has five main halls, as well as some stunning statuary. The path through the Lama Temple proceeds from south to north – from earth to heaven.

1 Hall of the Heavenly Kings
The first hall has a plump laughing Buddha, Milefo, back-to-back with Wei Tuo, the Guardian of Buddhist Doctrine. They are flanked by the Four Heavenly Kings.

Hall of Eternal Harmony 2
This, the second hall, contains three manifestations of Buddha **(right)** representing the past, present, and future. They are flanked by 18 *luohan* – those freed from the cycle of rebirth.

4 Hall of the Wheel of Dharma
Hall four has a large statue of Tsongkhapa, the 14th-century founder of the Yellow Hat sect of Buddhism. Dominant in Tibetan politics for centuries, the sect is led by the Dalai Lama and Panchen Lama.

6 Hall of Ten Thousand Happinesses
The final pavilion houses an 80-ft (25-m) high Buddha carved from a single piece of sandalwood. There's a splendid collection of Tibetan Buddhist objects in a room behind the hall.

3 Hall of Eternal Protection
The third hall **(above)** contains Buddhas of longevity and medicine, plus two *tangkas* said to have been embroidered by Emperor Qianlong's mother. Behind the hall is a bronze sculpture of Mount Meru.

5 Monks
At one time there were 1,500 monks at the temple; now there are only around 70. Although of the same Yellow Hat sect as the Dalai Lama, the monks are required to reject Tibetan independence.

7 Prayer Wheel
Spinning a prayer wheel sends a written prayer on coiled paper to heaven. A little yellow arrow taped to the frame of the wheel reminds worshipers that the wheel is to be spun in clockwise direction

8 Lion Statue

A large imperial lion **(left)** is a reminder that the complex was the residence of future Qing emperor Yongzheng. On ascending the throne in 1722, and in keeping with tradition, his former home became a temple.

PANCHEN LAMA

While the Dalai Lama, head of the sect to which the Lama Temple belongs, lives in exile, the second head, the Panchen Lama, resides in Beijing and recognizes Chinese authority. However, the matter of the true identity of the Panchen Lama is mired in controversy. China supports one candidate, while the Tibetans recognize another – only he vanished in suspicious circumstances in 1995. Later, in 2018, the Dalai Lama confirmed that the Panchen Lama was alive and well.

Lama Temple (Yonghe Gong)

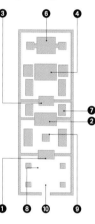

9 Incense Burner

There are incense burners **(below)** in front of all the many altars throughout the temple. Shops lining the entryway to the complex and in the neighboring streets are piled with bundles of incense sticks for sale for use at the temple.

10 Drum and Bell Towers

The temple's Drum and Bell towers are in the first courtyard after passing through the main entrance. The huge bell **(above)** has been removed from its tower and placed on the ground.

NEED TO KNOW

MAP F1 ■ 12 Yonghe Gong Dajie ■ 6404 1919 ■ Subway: Yonghe Gong Exit C

Open 9am–4.30pm daily (Nov–Mar: to 4pm)

Adm ¥25, audio guides ¥50 (plus ¥200 deposit)

■ The snacks at the kiosks are overpriced, so it is a good idea to bring your own refreshments.

■ Photography is not allowed within the halls, but you can take pictures of the exteriors and of the courtyards.

Following pages The blue-tiled Hall of Prayer for Good Harvests, Temple of Heaven

TOP 10 ⭐ Bei Hai Park

An imperial garden for over 1,000 years, Bei Hai was opened to the public in 1925. Filled with artificial hills, pavilions, and temples, it is associated with Kublai Khan, who redesigned it during the Mongol Yuan dynasty. These days, it is a fine place for a leisurely stroll, and a bit of boating on the lake.

1 **Round City**
Bei Hai was the site of Beijing's earliest imperial palace, although nothing now remains other than a small pavilion on a site known as the Round City, and a large jade wine vessel said to have belonged to Kublai Khan.

2 **The Place of Serenity**
In the northwest corner of the park is this utterly beautiful garden, created in the mid-18th century by the Qianlong emperor, with rockeries, pavilions, and ornate bridges over goldfish-filled pools.

3 **Three Temples**
Near the Place of Serenity is a trio of small temple buildings – the Pavilion of 10,000 Buddhas **(left)**, the Glazed Pavilion, which is covered with green and yellow ceramic Buddhas, and the Xiao Xitian (Small Western Sky) Temple filled with fearsome-looking idols.

4 **White Dagoba**
Topping Jade Island, this is a Tibetan-style stupa built to honor the visit of the fifth Dalai Lama in 1651. It has been rebuilt twice since.

PARK PLAY

Beijing's parks double as recreation centers, particularly for the city's elderly citizens. Early in the morning, they gather to perform *tai ji quan* (tai chi) exercises. Many then spend the rest of the day in the park playing cards or mahjong, engaging in *yang ge* (fan dancing) or ballroom dancing, or just reading the paper and talking with friends.

5 Jade Island
Accessed by bridge from the south gate or by boat from the north gate, Bei Hai's willow-lined island **(below)** was created from the earth excavated to form the lake.

9 Yongan Temple
Located beneath the Dagoba on Jade Island, this temple comprises a series of ascending halls, including the Hall of the Wheel of Law, with its central effigy of the Buddha Sakyamuni **(left)**.

7 Pavilion of Calligraphy
A crescent-shaped hall on Jade Island contains nearly 500 stone tablets engraved with the work of famous Chinese calligraphers. If the exhibits are less than enthralling, the walkways that lead to the pavilion are enchanting.

8 Zhong Nan Hai
Bei Hai means "North Lake"; the Middle (Zhong) and South (Nan) Lakes are part of an area occupied by China's political leaders and are off-limits to all except government officials. Zhong Nan Hai is regarded as the new Forbidden City.

10 Fangshan Restaurant
Founded in 1926 by chefs of the imperial household, the restaurant **(above)** bases its menus on court cuisine. Standards have slipped, but the opulent setting still has great appeal.

6 Nine Dragon Screen
This free-standing wall made of colorful glazed ceramic tiles depicts nine intertwined dragons **(above)**. The Chinese dragon is a beneficent beast offering protection and good luck. The wall was designed to obstruct the passage of evil spirits.

NEED TO KNOW

MAP K1 ■ 1 Wenjin Jie, Xicheng ■ 6403 3225 ■ info@beihaipark.com.cn ■ Subway: Beihai Bei or Tian'an Men West ■ Buses: 5, 101, 103, 107, 109, 111

Open 6:30am–9pm daily (Nov–Mar: to 8:30pm);

buildings close 5pm (Nov–Mar: 4pm)

Adm ¥10 (Nov–Mar ¥5); Yongan Temple and Round City cost an extra ¥10 each; combined ticket for park, Yongan Temple and Round City ¥20 (Nov–Mar ¥15)

■ There are snack kiosks in the park.

■ The park has four entry gates: the most convenient is the south gate, close to Forbidden City; the north gate is located across the road from Hou Hai, where there are good eateries.

Hou Hai

The area around the joined lakes of Qian Hai and Hou Hai has traditionally been home to nobles and wealthy merchants. Several grand homes survive, hidden in the labyrinthine old lanes known as *hutongs*. This is a rare quarter of Beijing where the 21st century is kept at bay, and these back alleys represent one of the most satisfying parts of the city to explore on foot – or by rickshaw.

① Boating and skating
In summer the lakes are filled with small pedal boats. By mid-December, they are frozen over **(below)** and a large area is cordoned off for ice-skating.

② Silver Ingot Bridge
The narrow channel that connects Hou Hai's two lakes is spanned by the pretty, arched Silver Ingot Bridge, which dates from the time of the Yuan dynasty (1279–1368).

③ Former Residence of Guo Moruo
Beijing's many "former residences of" are mostly connected with Party favorites. Moruo was an author and key figure in the rise of Communism in China.

④ Hutongs
The lakes **(above)** lie at the heart of a sprawling old district, characterized by traditional alleyways known as *hutongs*. These alleys are lined for the most part by the blank outer walls of *siheyuan*, which are inward-looking houses arranged around a central courtyard.

⑤ Drum and Bell Towers
Just north of the eastern end of Yandai Xie Jie, these two imposing towers *(see p81)* once marked the northernmost limits of the city. You can ascend the towers for views of Hou Hai.

NEED TO KNOW

MAP D2 ■ Subway: Shicha Hai, Jishuitan, Beihai North

Mansion of Prince Gong: 8328 8149; open Apr–Oct: 8am–6:30pm daily, Nov–Mar: 9am–6:30pm Tue–Sun; adm ¥40 (¥70 with tour guide, tea and snack tasting, and traditional opera performance; call ahead for times); www.pgm.org.cn

Former Residence of Guo Moruo: 6612 5984; open 9am–4.30pm Tue–Sun; closed Dec 25 until 5th day of Chinese New Year; adm ¥20

Song Qingling's Residence: 6404 4205; open Apr–Oct: 9am–5:30pm daily (Nov–Mar: to 4:30pm); adm ¥20

■ Visit Hou Hai by day to explore the *hutongs* and historic residences, but come back later to dine and see the lake glimmering with the flotilla of tea-candles floated out on the water each evening.

■ The Hou Hai area has several excellent bars and restaurants *(see pp84–5)*.

8 Rickshaw tours

One way of seeing the *hutongs* is from a rickshaw **(left)**. Prices are negotiable, but expect to pay around ¥180 per person for a two-hour jaunt with the occasional stop-off.

Hou Hai

10 Mansion of Prince Gong

This former residence of Prince Gong is a preserved historic mansion in Beijing. The garden is a pattern of corridors and pavilions, dotted with pools and gates **(below)**.

6 Song Qingling's Residence

Song Qingling was the wife of the revolutionary leader Sun Yat Sen. Her former living quarters are now a small museum. The surrounding gardens are beautiful.

9 Yandai Xie Jie

One of the busiest tourist streets in Beijing, Yandai Xie Jie is lined with historic buildings, most of which have been converted into small bars and boutiques, including a temple that now functions as a café.

7 Lotus Lane

This is Hou Hai's main lakeside parade of restaurants, bars, and cafés **(below)**. Many of these establishments boast attractive waterfront terraces.

SIHEYUAN

Traditional Beijing homes, known as *siheyuan,* are arranged around a central courtyard. Originally homes of the well-to-do, over time many *siheyuan* were occupied by poorer families, who squeezed several households into the space formerly occupied by one. Modernization has destroyed many of these dwellings, but there is a movement to preserve those that have survived. A few of them have recently been converted into hotels.

TOP 10 ⭐ Summer Palace (Yiheyuan)

A vast landscaped park on the edge of the city, this seasonal imperial retreat from the stifling confines of the Forbidden City was the favored haunt of Empress Cixi. She had it rebuilt twice: once after its destruction by French and English troops in 1860, and again in 1902, after it was plundered during the Boxer Rebellion.

1 Hall of Happiness and Longevity

This impressive hall was the residence of the Empress Cixi. It has supposedly been left just as it was at the time of her death in 1908, complete with its Qing dynasty-era furniture.

2 Garden of Virtue and Harmony

This pretty complex of roofed corridors, small pavilions, rock gardens, and pools also includes Cixi's private three-story theater. The buildings now contain Qing-era artifacts, from vehicles to costumes and glassware.

3 Long Corridor

From the Hall of Happiness and Longevity the rather aptly named Long Corridor **(left)** zigzags along the shore of the lake, interrupted along its length by four pavilions. The corridor's ceilings and beams are decorated with over 14,000 scenic paintings.

Summer Palace (Yiheyuan

Kunming Lake

West Lake

Nanhu Lake

KUN MING HU LU

KUN MING HU DONG LU

4 Tower of the Fragrance of the Buddha

Toward the peak of Longevity Hill rises this octagonal tower. The stiff climb is rewarded with views over the roofs of the halls and pavilions to the lake below.

7 Temple of the Sea of Wisdom

North of the Fragrance of the Buddha Tower is a tiled temple decorated with glazed Buddhist effigies, many of which have sadly been vandalized **(left)**.

5 Longevity Hill

At around the half-way point of the Long Corridor, a series of buildings ascends the slopes of Longevity Hill **(below)**. The start of the sequence is marked at the lakeside by a fine decorative gate.

EMPRESS CIXI

Cixi is remembered as one of China's most powerful women. Having borne one emperor's son as an imperial concubine, she became the power behind the throne to two more: her son and her nephew. When she blocked state reforms and lent support to the xenophobic Boxers in their rebellion, she unwittingly paved the way for the end of the imperial era.

8 Seventeen-Arch Bridge

South Lake Island is linked to the eastern shore by a bridge **(below)** with a lion crowning each of the 544 balusters along its length, all supposedly individual. An impressive-looking bronze ox rests on the eastern shore.

6 Suzhou Street

This shopping street was built for the amusement of the Qianlong emperor, his concubines and eunuchs, who would play at being shoppers, shopkeepers, and pickpockets.

NEED TO KNOW

6 miles (10 km) NW of central Beijing ■ 6288 1144 ■ Subway: Bagou, then bus 394; Bei Gong Men ■ www.summer palace-china.com

Open Apr–Oct: 6:30am–8pm (park) daily, 8:30am–5pm (sights) daily; Nov–Mar: 7am–7pm (park) daily, 9am– 4pm (sights) daily; the last admission is two hours before closing

Adm ¥60 all inclusive (Nov–Mar ¥50); ¥30 park only (Nov–Mar ¥25); audio guides are available for ¥40 (plus ¥50 deposit)

■ There are several small snack kiosks situated in the park grounds.

■ Avoid visiting on days with poor visibility when you risk missing the superb views across the Summer Palace lake.

9 South Lake Island

Crowning this island on Kunming Lake is the Dragon King Temple (Longwang Miao), which is dedicated to the god of rivers, seas, and rain.

10 Marble Boat

The wooden structure of the boat is painted white to look like marble. Boat trips to South Lake Island depart from a neighboring jetty.

798 Art District

TOP 10

Since the first artists set up in Da Shan Zi's newly vacated 798 factory in 2001, the East German-built industrial compound has become a world-famous center of contemporary Chinese art. Alongside the studios and galleries, there are also chic cafés, bars, and restaurants, not to mention a growing number of designer shops and showrooms. These days the area is popular with tourists, who arrive by the coachload.

Maoist graffiti
1 When many of the abandoned factory spaces in the district were being converted and refurbished for use as art galleries, the artists instructed the decorators to leave untouched the giant Maoist slogans that had been lettered on the walls by the former workers at the 798 factory.

Vibrant graffiti art in the 798 Art District

798 Photo Gallery
3 In addition to regularly changing exhibitions of work by both Chinese and foreign photographers, this gallery (left) also has a couple of mezzanine levels where a selection of photographic prints for sale are displayed.

Red Gate Gallery
2 This is Beijing's first privately-owned contemporary art gallery. It may have moved from its original location, but still promotes young Chinese artists and international cultural exchange, and hosts monthly-changing exhibitions and occasional art discussions.

AT Café
4 Once an arty canteen, this is now a fashionable café (right) whose notable feature is a bare-brick wall punctured by massive holes. A variety of pizzas and sandwiches, and fantastic coffee are served here.

Galleria Continua
5 Beijing's outpost of this Italian gallery, in a former munitions factory, aims to stimulate cultural exchanges. It hosts shows by renowned international artists such as Chen Zhen, Antony Gormley, Daniel Buren, and Anish Kapoor.

798 Art District

JIU XIAN QIAO BEI LU
707 ST
706 ST
705 ST
ROAD
797
798 MIDDLE 1ST ST
718 ST
798 WEST ST
798 MIDDLE 2ND ST
1ST ST
798 EAST ST
JIU XIAN QIAO LU
798 ROAD
QIXING RD
AIRPORT EXPRESSWAY

BRAVE NEW WORLDS

1985 marked the arrival of the avant garde in Chinese art, with controversial student graduation shows igniting intense debate in artistic circles. A year later, a New York gallery introduced the new Chinese art to an international audience. Today, China's art market is the third largest in the world.

⑦ UCCA

The Ullens Center for Contemporary Art (UCCA) is the largest single venue in this area, and exhibits an eclectic range of unconventional Chinese art **(below)**. UCCA has an auditorium for lectures and films, a store, and a restaurant.

⑨ Pace

This glamorous global gallery in the 798 Art District showcases the upper echelon of Chinese and Western contemporary art, and it also hosts Beijing Voice, an annual East-West art discussion between industry elites.

⑥ Timezone 8

This is a trendy Western and Japanese restaurant that serves imported beers, saké and *sochu*. It boasts a pleasant terrace, ideal for people-watching, and excellent air-con inside.

⑧ Beijing Commune

This Bauhaus-style brick building has been promoting aspiring Chinese artists since 2004. It primarily focuses on solo performances.

⑩ Magician Space

This small avant-garde gallery with a pioneering spirit has hosted a solo exhibition by the controversial Chinese artist Ai Weiwei.

NEED TO KNOW

2–4 Jiu Xian Qiao Lu, Da Shan Zi, Chaoyang
■ Subway: Jiangtai, then walk north for 15 min
■ Bus: 401, 402, 405, 418, 445, 955, 973, 988, 991

To Caochangdi: Bus 418 from Dong Zhi Men

Galleria Continua: 5978 9505; open 11am–6pm

Tue–Sun; www.galleria continua.com

UCCA: 5780 0200; open 10am–7pm Tue–Sun; adm ¥60 (free on Thu); www.ucca.org.cn

Beijing Commune: 8456 2862; open 10am–6pm Tue–Sat; www.beijingcommune.com

Pace: 5978 9781; open 10am–6pm Tue–Sat; www.pacegallery.com

Magician Space: 5978 9635; open 10:30am–6:30pm Tue–Sun; magician-space.com

■ The Ullens Center for Contemporary Art provides free maps of the entire 798 area. Most galleries are open from around 11am to 7pm, and are closed on Mondays.

⭐ Ming Tombs

The resting place for 13 of the 16 Ming-dynasty (1368–1644) emperors, this is China's finest example of imperial funerary architecture. The site was chosen because of its auspicious feng shui alignment: a ridge of mountains to the north cradles the tombs on three sides, protecting the dead from the evil spirits carried on the north wind. The tombs are spread over 15 square miles (40 sq km). Three (Chang Ling, Ding Ling, and Zhao Ling) have been restored and are often busy. The others are not open to the public.

1 Stele Pavilion
At the tunnel-like arch of the Stele Pavilion, the largest stele in China projects from the shell of a giant bixi (dragon-tortoise) and bears the names of the emperors buried at the site.

3 Spirit Tower
Rising up from the third courtyard of the Chang Ling complex, this tower marks the entrance to the burial chamber. It takes the form of an earthen tumulus girdled by a wall.

2 Memorial Arch
Marking the entrance to the site is a five-arched marble gate (above) built in 1540. At 40 ft (12 m) high and more than 92 ft (28 m) wide, it is the largest of its kind in China, and boasts beautiful carvings.

4 Ding Ling Treasures
A collection of precious artifacts and relics from the Wanli emperor's tomb (the Ding Ling) have been placed in the Hall of Eminent Favor.

NEED TO KNOW

30 miles (45 km) NW of Beijing ▪ 6076 1424 ▪ Subway to Changping Dongguan station, then bus 314 to Changling or Dingling station ▪ www.mingtombs.com

Open Apr–Oct 8am–5:30pm daily; Nov–Mar 8:30am–5pm daily

Adm Chang Ling ¥45 (¥30 off-peak), Ding Ling ¥60 (¥40 off-peak), Zhao Ling ¥30 (¥20 off-peak); Combo ticket ¥130 (¥100 off-peak)

▪ The Ming Tombs can most conveniently be covered as part of a trip to the Great Wall at Badaling. Many hotels are able to arrange tours to the site.

▪ Bus 872 leaves Desheng Men Bus Terminal every 10 minutes (9:15am–4:15pm) to Changling and Dingling (¥10). The last return bus is at 3pm.

▪ There are snack kiosks available at the site.

Ming Tombs

5 Chang Ling Tomb

The resting place **(below)** of the Yongle emperor, builder of the Forbidden City and Temple of Heaven, is the oldest and grandest tomb. It is well restored, but the chamber where Yongle, his wife, and 16 concubines are buried has never been excavated.

7 Zhao Ling Tomb

This is the final resting place of the Longqing emperor (1537–72). The 13th emperor of the Ming dynasty, he gained the throne at the age of 30 and died six years later. The tomb has an attractive triple-bridge built over a stream. It is closed for renovation.

9 Spirit Way

Part of the 4-mile (7-km) approach to the tombs, the Spirit Way is lined with 18 pairs of giant guardians **(above)** – stone statues of imperial warriors, court officials, animals, and Chinese mythical beasts.

10 Ding Ling Burial Chamber

This is the only burial chamber to be excavated and opened to the public. It holds three red-lacquer coffins, belonging to Wanli and his two wives.

6 Ding Ling Tomb

This is the tomb of the longest-reigning Ming emperor, Wanli (1573–1620). His profligate rule initiated the downfall of the dynasty. His tomb **(below)** took six years to build, and its impressive structure is representative of the emperor's extravagant lifestyle.

8 Hall of Eminent Favor

One of China's most impressive surviving Ming buildings, this double-eaved sacrificial hall is the centerpiece of the Chang Ling tomb complex. It stands on a triple-tiered marble terrace and 32 gigantic cedar columns support its hipped roof.

THE MING DYNASTY

The 276-year Ming ("brilliant") dynasty rule was one of the longest and most stable periods in Chinese history. The founder of the Ming dynasty rose from humble beginnings via military successes to become emperor. He was succeeded by his grandson, who in turn was succeeded by his son, who proclaimed himself emperor Yongle ("Eternal Joy"). It was Yongle who moved the capital from Nanjing to Beijing, where he created a new city.

TOP 10 ⭐ Great Wall of China

The Great Wall of China snakes over deserts, hills, and plains for several thousand miles. At its closest point it is less than 40 miles (65 km) from Beijing. Created after the unification of China under Qin Shi Huangdi (221–210 BC), it ultimately proved ineffective; it was breached in the 13th century by the Mongols and again, in the 17th century, by the Manchus. There are four main sites accessible from Beijing: Badaling, Mutianyu, Huanghua Cheng, and Simatai.

1 Badaling

The restored Ming fortification at Badaling is the closest section of the wall to Beijing. Its accessibility means it is perpetually busy, but it is possible to escape the crowds by walking along the wall. Opt for a cable-car ride and enjoy the spectacular views.

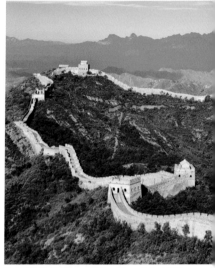

Great Wall of China snaking through lush hills

2 Great Wall Museum

Housed in an imitation Qing dynasty building at Badaling, this museum **(left)** presents the entire history of the region from Neolithic times, as well as details about the construction of the wall.

3 Commune by the Great Wall

Near the wall at Badaling, the Commune consists of 12 villas, each designed by a different Asian architect. The complex operates as a hotel, but non-guests can drop by for lunch, or take a tour.

NEED TO KNOW

Badaling: 44 miles (70 km) NW of Beijing; 6912 1383; bus 879 from Badaling; open 6:30am–7pm daily (Nov–Mar: 7am–6pm daily); adm ¥45

Xizhazi (Jiankou): 60 miles (96 km) N of Beijing; bus 936 from Dong Zhi Men bus station, to Yujiayuan station, then bus H25 to Xizhazi station

Mutianyu: 56 miles (90 km) N of Beijing; 6162 6505; bus 916 from Dong Zhi Men station, change at Huairou; open 7:30am–6pm Mon–Fri, 7:30am–6:30pm Sat & Sun (Nov–Mar: 8am–5pm daily); adm ¥40

Huanghua Cheng: 37 miles (60 km) N of Beijing; 6165 1044; bus 916 to Huairou station, then bus H21 to Small West Lake station; open 8.30am–5pm Mon–Fri, 8am–6pm Sat & Sun (Nov–Mar: 8:30am–4:30pm daily); adm ¥45

Juyong Guan: open 8am–5pm daily (Nov–Mar: 8.30am–4pm daily); adm ¥45 (Nov–Mar: ¥40)

4 Juyong Guan

This pass is on the way to Badaling. With unscalable mountains on either side it is easy to see why the spot was chosen for defence. Early cannons remain on the ramparts. Also worth seeing are Buddhist carvings on a stone platform, or "cloud terrace," in the middle of the pass.

VISITING THE WALL

Most hotels are able to organize a trip to the wall, usually combined with a visit to the Ming Tombs *(see pp32–3)*. Try to find out whether there are any unwanted diversions to jade factories, cloisonné workshops, or Chinese medicine clinics. Small groups can see more remote parts of the wall, by hiring a taxi for the day from Beijing. Hiking clubs in Beijing offer day trips to lesser-known parts of the wall.

7 Xizhazi

This village in the less-developed Jiankou area affords spectacular views and accessible hikes. Xizhazi's local guesthouses offer fresh, country-style dining and a night on a traditional *kang* (heated bed).

5 Gubeikou

Once called Simatai village, this area has been redeveloped as Gubeikou, or "Water Town." It is a 7-mile (12-km) walk to Jinshanling, taking around five hours.

8 Shanhaiguan

The wall ends (or begins) at the sea **(above)**. East of town, the "First Pass Under Heaven" is a formidable section of wall attached to a gatehouse. A good destination if you want to do an overnight trip.

9 Mutianyu

In a dramatic hilly setting, and with a series of watchtowers along its restored length, the wall here dates from 1368. Local village buildings have now been converted into both holiday homes and restaurants.

6 Jinshanling

This is the starting point for a steep and stony hike to Gubeikou. However, the path may be blocked due to restoration work. The views **(below)** as the wall winds over the sharp peaks are fantastic.

10 Huanghua Cheng

On the same stretch of wall as Mutianyu, Huanghua Cheng is an exhilarating section of Ming fortifications that is far less developed and crowded than most other parts. The great barrier is split into two by a large reservoir. The crumbling masonry can be uneven and fairly treacherous, so you need to take care.

The Top 10 of Everything

**Performers on stage during
a Beijing Opera show**

⏱**10** Moments in History

① 500,000 BC: Peking Man Hunts and Gathers

Unearthed in the 1920s from a cave at Zhoukoudian, 30 miles (45 km) south-west of Beijing, 40-odd fossilized bones and primitive implements were identified as the remains of Peking Man *(Homo erectus Pekinensis)*, who lived in the vicinity over 500,000 years ago.

Kublai Khan, of the Mongol Yuan dynasty

② 1215: Genghis Khan Sacks Zhongdu

The future Beijing was developed as an auxiliary capital under the Liao (907–1125) and Jin (1115–1234) dynasties, at which time it was known as Zhongdu. In 1215 it was invaded and razed by a Mongol army led by the fearsome Genghis Khan.

③ Late 13th Century: Marco Polo Visits

Under the Mongol Yuan dynasty's first emperor, Kublai Khan (r. 1260–94), the city became known as Khanbalik, and was one of twin capitals – the other was Yuanshangdu, or Xanadu – of the largest empire ever known.

The Venetian traveler Marco Polo was dazzled by the imperial palace: "No man on earth could design anything superior to it."

④ 1403–20: Construction of the Forbidden City

The Ming emperor Yongle (r. 1403–24) destroyed the palaces of his Mongol predecessors in order to rebuild the city, which he renamed Beijing (Northern Capital). He is credited with laying the foundations for the city as it is today, and the Forbidden City and Temple of Heaven began to take shape during his reign.

⑤ 1900: Boxer Rebellion

Western powers, frustrated by the reluctance of the Chinese to open up to foreign trade, put the imperial court under pressure, eventually going to war to protect their trade in opium. In 1900, championed by the Empress Cixi, a band of rebels known as the Boxers attacked Beijing's Foreign Legation Quarter. A joint eight-nation army had to be sent to lift the siege.

Violent clashes during the Boxer Rebellion of 1900

1912: The End of Empire
The last emperor, Pu Yi, was only three years old when he ascended the throne. Four years later, in February 1912, he was forced to abdicate by general Yuan Shikai's new National Assembly.

7 1949: Founding of the People's Republic of China
In January 1949, Communist forces led by Mao Zedong seized Beijing. On October 1, Mao proclaimed the People's Republic of China from the gallery of the Tian'an Men.

Mao's 1965 Cultural Revolution

8 1965: Launch of the Cultural Revolution
Having socialized industry and agriculture, Mao called on the masses to transform society itself. All distinctions between manual and intellectual work were to be abolished and the class system was to be eradicated. The revolution reached its violent peak in 1967, with the Red Guards spreading fear and havoc.

9 1976: The Death of Mao
On September 9, 1976 Mao died. His long-time opponent Deng Xiaoping became leader, implementing reforms that encouraged greater economic freedom.

10 2008: Beijing Hosts the Olympics
In 2008, Beijing hosted the Olympic Games. The city revamped its infrastructures, and some of the most striking and innovative buildings were created to house the various competitions (see pp44–5).

TOP 10 CHINESE INVENTIONS

Chinese magnetic compass

1 Magnetic compass
Developed from an instrument used for *feng shui* and geomancy, it helped the Chinese explore the world.

2 Printing
In the 11th century, the Chinese carved individual characters on pieces of clay, inventing movable block type.

3 Paper money
This was developed by Chinese merchants as certificates of exchange. Lighter than coins, bills were soon adopted by the government.

4 Gunpowder
Stumbled on by Daoist alchemists seeking the elixir of life.

5 Seismometer
A ball fell from one of four dragons' mouths to indicate the direction of the earthquake.

6 Abacus
Invented during the Yuan dynasty and still in use throughout China today.

7 Porcelain
The Chinese invented porcelain 1,000 years before Europe caught on – and kept production methods secret to protect their competitive advantage.

8 Paper
A prototype paper was made from mulberry bark, although bamboo, hemp, linen, and silk were also used to write on.

9 Crossbow
Better range, accuracy, and penetration than the standard bow.

10 Decimal system
Developed alongside the writing system, the decimal system led to mathematical advances.

🔟 Places of Worship

Pavilion in the Confucius Temple

a variety of languages including Mandarin, English and Latin. Service times are posted on the noticeboard.

③ St. Joseph's Church

MAP N3 ■ 74 Wangfujing Dajie ■ 6524 0634 ■ Subway: Dengshikou

Also known as the East Cathedral, this is a triple-domed church in the Baroque style. It was first built on the site of the residence of a Jesuit missionary in 1655 and, following earthquakes, fire, and the destruction wrought during the Boxer Rebellion, has had to be rebuilt on a number of occasions since. It is fronted by a gateway and piazza, and is beautifully lit at night. Mass is held in English on Sundays at 4pm.

① Confucius Temple (Kong Miao)

An enormous complex of wooden halls and flagstoned courtyards, the Confucius Temple (see p82) is popular with visitors and pays testament to the revival of Confucian ethics in modern China. A museum inside the temple holds artifacts of the Imperial civil service exams, and Confucian texts.

② South Cathedral

Officially known as the Cathedral of the Immaculate Conception, this (see p76) was the first Catholic house of worship in Beijing. It is the largest functioning church, and has regular services in

Incense burner at Wanshou Temple

④ Wanshou Temple

MAP A1 ■ Xisanhuan Lu, on the north side of Zizhu Qiao Bridge ■ 6842 3565 ■ Subway: Xizhi Men, then bus 300, 360, or 361 ■ Open 9am–4pm Tue–Sun ■ Adm

In the northwest Haidian District, the Wanshou (Longevity) Temple is worth a stop en route to the Summer Palace. The complex houses the Beijing Art Museum – a collection of historical relics including bronzes, jade, carved lacquer, and a small but exquisite collection of Buddha images.

⑤ White Cloud Temple

Founded in AD 739, this is Beijing's largest Daoist shrine (see p95). Daoism, also known as Taoism, is a Chinese folk religion, which centers around maintaining a positive relationship with several categories of gods, ghosts, and ancestral spirits.

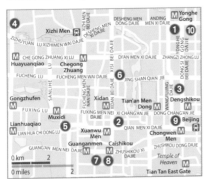

Facade of the Gothic North Cathedral

6 North Cathedral
MAP J2 ■ 33 Xishiku Dajie
■ Subway: Xisi

The white-trimmed blue facade of this cathedral, a twin-towered piece of Gothic confectionery, masks a bloody past: not long after the Jesuits finished the church in 1889, it came under siege during the Boxer Rebellion. Many of the congregation sheltering inside were killed.

7 Niu Jie Mosque
There are about 200,000 Muslims in Beijing. The majority live in the Niu Jie District, which is a busy area with halal butchers, bakers, and restaurants. The mosque *(see p76)* is the city's oldest and largest Islamic place of worship. Despite being over 1,000 years old, the mosque looks splendid, having been renovated to the tune of $2.4 million.

8 Fayuan Temple
This temple *(see p74)* doubles as a Buddhist Academy. Founded in 1956, the Academy trains monks to serve in monasteries throughout China. The temple has an excellent collection of sculptures, including a giant reclining Buddha.

9 St. Michael's Church
MAP N5 ■ 13 Dong Jiao Min Xiang ■ 6513 5170 ■ Subway: Chongwen Men

This is one of the city's lesser-known churches, hidden away in the old Legation Quarter *(see p76)*. It was built in 1901, with three Gothic spires, to serve the area's various embassies. Narrowly escaping destruction during the Cultural Revolution, it was renovated by the Chinese Patriotic Catholic Church, to whom it now belongs.

10 Lama Temple
One of the most notable centers of Buddhism outside Tibet until it was shut down during the Cultural Revolution, this temple *(see pp20–21)* was reputedly saved from destruction by the intervention of the then president, Zhou Enlai. The precincts are home to around 70 monks.

Gilded statues at the Lama Temple, an important Buddhist center

TOP 10 Museums

3 Songtang Museum

MAP F1 ■ 3 Guozijian Jie ■ Subway: Yonghe Gong ■ Open 9am–6pm daily ■ Adm

A Cultural Revolution survivor, Li Songtang wanted to preserve ancient China from both political and economic destruction. Housed in a 200-year-old *hutong* courtyard home, this museum displays stone and wood carvings, plus a number of artifacts from several dynasties.

1 National Museum of China

What the British Museum is to London, the National Museum of China *(see p70)* is to Beijing. Dedicated to Chinese history and arts, it documents the evolution of Chinese civilization through the country's most important historic and cultural artifacts. The museum hosts two permanent, and numerous temporary exhibitions of art, history, and archaeology.

4 Poly Art Museum

MAP G2 ■ Floor 9, New Poly Plaza, 1 Chaoyang Men Bei Dajie, Dongcheng District ■ 6500 1188 ■ Open 9:30am–4:30pm Mon–Sat ■ Adm

This museum is cool, quiet, and packed with ancient Chinese bronzes and Buddhist statuary.

5 Imperial City Art Museum

Call by this museum near the Forbidden City *(see p70)* to see all the bits of imperial Beijing that didn't survive. The walls and gates that once encircled the city, along with dozens of vanished temples, are revisited through a great many maps, models, and photographs.

6 Beijing Police Museum

MAP M6 ■ 36 Dong Jiao Min Xiang ■ 8522 5018 ■ Subway: Qian Men ■ Open 9am–4pm Tue–Sun

In the 19th-century former City Bank of New York, this surprisingly fun museum has displays on themes such as the suppression of drug dealers and counter-revolutionaries. Famed police dog Feisheng is stuffed and mounted and there are live transmissions from a traffic camera. An interactive screen poses questions and correct answers win prizes.

Natural History Museum

2 Natural History Museum

The museum *(see p77)* has around 5,000 specimens on display, including a fine collection of models and skeletons of dinosaurs, and other prehistoric creatures.

The modern building housing the Capital Museum

7 Capital Museum

Formerly housed in the Confucius Temple, this museum *(see p94)* now boasts a large and modern five-story building near Fuxingmen. It documents Beijing's history through over 200,000 relics and archival images. Among the many permanent exhibitions is the fascinating "Stories of the Capital City – Old Beijing Folk Customs".

8 National Art Museum of China

The largest art museum in the country, with an impressive 64,580 sq ft (6,000 sq m) of floor space, the National Art Museum of China *(see p70)* hosts several exhibitions which feature inter-nationally renowned Chinese and foreign artists. Memorable shows have included an ethnic textile exhibition and a display by famed Mexican photographer Pedro Meyer.

National Art Museum of China

9 Ancient Architecture Museum

Close to the Temple of Heaven, south of Tian'an Men Square, this place *(see p77)* is worth a visit for the museum building alone, which is the pavilion of a former grand temple complex.

Ground floor at the Military Museum

10 Military Museum of the Chinese People's Revolution

Visitors to this museum *(see p96)* are greeted by paintings of Mao, Marx, Lenin, and Stalin, at least two of whom were responsible for inflicting the horrific levels of death and destruction depicted within the museum. The first floor is filled with fighter planes, tanks, and missiles, while displays upstairs chronicle China's military campaigns.

TOP 10 The Olympic Legacy

The iconic architecture of the National Olympic Stadium (Bird's Nest)

1 Digital Beijing Building

Designed by Beijing-based Studio Pei Zhu, Digital Beijing served as the Games' Control and Data Center. It resembles a barcode from one side and an integrated circuit board from the other. It now accommodates a virtual museum and an exhibition center.

National Aquatics Center/Water Cube

2 National Aquatics Center/Water Cube

Inspired by bubbles and molecules, the dramatic-looking Water Cube (see p49) is a complex of five pools. After the Olympic Games, it was transformed into a giant water park with slides and a wave pool.

3 National Indoor Stadium

Built to host gymnastics and handball during the 2008 Games, this stadium boasts a curving roof with slatted beams, inspired by Chinese folding fans. Post-Olympics, it stages entertainment events.

4 National Olympic Stadium (Bird's Nest)

Designed in collaboration with the Chinese artist Ai Weiwei, the National Olympic Stadium is an architectural icon. Its outer ribbons of structural steel resemble the woven twigs of a bird's nest as they loop and swirl over the 91,000-seat arena, hence the building's nickname.

5 Olympic Green

The vast Olympic Green surrounds the Olympic Village and extends beyond the fifth ring road. At its heart is a dragon-shaped lake, as well as waterfalls, meadows, and streams. Entry is free.

6 Olympic Green Convention Center

This building hosted the fencing events during the Games, as well as providing a home for the International Broadcasting Center. Its distinctive shape mirrors the traditional Chinese "flying roof" and acts as a giant rainwater collector. The building is now a multipurpose conference center.

7 Beijing Airport, Terminal 3

One of the world's largest and most advanced airport buildings, Lord Norman Foster's Terminal 3 welcomed international athletes to the 2008 Olympics. The design resembles a soaring dragon in red and yellow, thus evoking traditional Chinese colors and symbols.

8️⃣ National Center for the Performing Arts
MAP K5

French architect Paul Andreu's silvery "Egg" *(see p70)* provides a striking contrast to the monolithic Socialist architecture of neighboring Tian'an Men Square. The building is surrounded by a reflective moat and accessed by an underwater tunnel. A part of the facade is transparent, so at night passers-by can see inside.

9️⃣ LeSports Center

Rebranded since the Olympics, the host venue for the basketball games features a unique exterior design that gives the impression of movement, with boards alternately rising and falling. More than mere show, the aluminum alloy boards reflect heat and reportedly result in 60–70 per cent energy savings. The facility has a capacity to seat 18,000 people and is one of Beijing's largest.

🔟 CCTV Building
MAP H4

The most striking addition to the Beijing skyline is the headquarters of China Central Television. Designed by Dutch architects Rem Koolhaas and Ole Scheeren, it is a gravity-defying loop that pushes the limits of architecture. Its unusual design has prompted some locals to nickname the building "Glass Pants" (trousers).

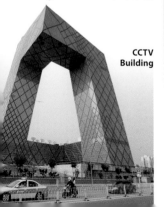

CCTV Building

TOP 10 SOCIALIST MONUMENTS

Great Hall of the People

1 Great Hall of the People
MAP L5
Over 300 rooms built in 10 months.

2 Agricultural Exhibition Center
MAP H2
In 1959, for the tenth anniversary of the People's Republic of China, this was one of ten buildings commissioned.

3 National Museum of China
MAP M5
This museum is every bit as brutal and ugly as the Great Hall, which it faces across the square.

4 Beijing Railway Station
MAP F4
Prime illustration of 1959's "size is everything" approach to architecture.

5 Cultural Palace of the Nationalities
MAP C4
The one "tenth-anniversary" building of elegance. Its plan forms the Chinese character for "mountain."

6 Minzu Hotel
MAP C4
No Chinese motifs here – but it's suitably monolithic and drab.

7 Military Museum of the Chinese People's Revolution
MAP A4
Owes a striking debt to Moscow.

8 Natural History Museum
MAP E6
Neo-Classical Socialist Chinese – but fairly nice once you're inside.

9 National Art Museum of China
MAP M2
The largest art gallery in China.

10 Beijing West Railway Station
MAP A5
A 1995 take on 1959-style architecture.

🔟 Off The Beaten Path

1 White Cloud Temple

Built in AD 739, Beijing's only Taoist temple *(see p95)* houses the China Taoist Association and 30 monks with their distinctive navy-blue robes and top knots. It usually sees more pilgrims than tourists and has elaborate halls and gates, as well as three stone monkeys – finding them all is said to bring good luck.

Inside the Watermelon Museum

2 The Watermelon Museum

Pangge Zhuang Town, Daxing District ■ 8928 1181 ■ Subway: Huangcun Xidajie ■ Open 10am–5pm Mon–Fri ■ Adm

Located to the south of Beijing, the Watermelon Museum is a surrealist modern Socialist museum. China is the world's biggest exporter of watermelons, and self-pick farms surround this gleaming temple to the famous fruit. Although there aren't any signs in English anywhere, you can get the gist of the exhibits.

3 Ancient Observatory

Located in a watchtower, this is one of the world's oldest observatories *(see p89)*. Among the many artifacts on display here are replicas of the old navigational tools that enabled Ming dynasty travelers to explore the world.

Sundial, Ancient Observatory

4 Beijing Shijingshan Amusement Park

Shijingshan Road, Shijingshan District ■ 8892 5159 ■ Subway: Bajiao Amusement Park ■ Open 9am–4:30pm daily (to 5pm Sat & Sun) ■ Adm; free for children under 6 years or 4 ft (1.2 m)

Beijing's oldest amusement park may not have the high-tech rides and high profile of the newer ones, but it is considerably cheaper, and less crowded. The rides here are fun nonetheless, and it has a certain faded-grandeur and kitsch charm. The park is divided into themed districts offering several entertainment facilities, including parades, shows and performances.

5 Beijing Botanical Gardens

If the hustle and bustle of the city gets to be too much, surround yourself with Chinese roses, peach blossoms, and peonies. The massive greenhouse here *(see p100)* displays more than 3,000 varieties of flora, ranging from tropical to desert.

Beijing Botanical Gardens in full bloom

Bronze lion at Fayuan Temple

9 Poly Art Museum

The silent, richly carpeted rooms at the Poly Art Museum (*see p40*) hold a wealth of stone, ceramic, and bronze statuary. Highlights include four bronze animals rescued from the 19th-century sacking of the Summer Palace, as well as artifacts ranging from the Shang to the Tang dynasties and earlier.

10 Beijing Eunuch Museum (Tian Yi Mu)

80 Moshi Kou Dajie, Shijing Shan District ▪ 8872 4148 ▪ Subway: Pingguoyuan, then bus 959 or 746 to Shougang Xiaoqu ▪ Open 8:30am–4:30pm daily ▪ Adm

In the 16th century, the eunuch Tian Yi, who carried his genitals in a jug, served three emperors of the Ming dynasty. Over time, he achieved an elevated position at court, and when he died, in 1605, his funeral generated three days of silence in the Forbidden City. Tian Yi's elaborately carved tomb is now empty, having been raided during China's Cultural Revolution. However, this interesting museum houses a range of murals, monuments, marble phalluses, and a diorama of unfortunate men about to undergo the unkindest cut.

6 Fayuan Temple

A visit to Fayuan Temple (*see p74*) offers the opportunity to observe the fascinating daily life of a monk. Built in AD 696 by Tang dynasty emperor Tai Zong to mourn fallen soldiers, Fayuan is Beijing's largest – and likely oldest – Buddhist temple.

7 Qianding Old Liquor Museum

MAP E2 ▪ 69 Zhaofu Jie (near Gulou), Dongcheng District ▪ 6404 0299 ▪ Subway: Gulou Dajie ▪ Open 9am–6pm Tue–Sun ▪ Adm

This museum is all about *baijiu* (traditional grain alcohol) through the ages, and on display are more than 1,600 varieties of the stuff. The entrance is tricky to find – look for the bottles embedded in brick.

8 The Former Residence of Guo Moruo

Guo Moruo was a 20th-century writer, poet, dramatist, historian, archeologist, and paleographer, as well as an enthusiastic gardener. Much of his outdoor handiwork survives here (*see p26*), his former home, in addition to piles of manuscripts, books, and a bronze statue of the man himself.

Children's Attractions

Display at the Natural History Museum

1 Natural History Museum

As long as you steer them clear of the partially dissected human bodies, children will love this place, with its animatronic dinosaurs, prehistoric skeletons, and stuffed animals of all sizes *(see p77)*.

2 Latitude

Anping Street, Houshayu, near Beijing Capital International Airport ▪ 8047 6556 ▪ Subway: Houshayu ▪ Open 10am–9pm Mon–Fri, 9am–10pm Sat & Sun ▪ Adm

Ideal for older kids, this indoor gym features trampolining, rock climbing, beam battle and dodge ball amongst a host of other thrilling activities. A great way to get the whole family active.

3 Beijing Aquarium

Located in the northeastern corner of the zoo, this is a very impressive attraction that will keep children happy for hours *(see p97)*.

4 New China Children's Store

MAP N4 ▪ 168 Wangfujing Dajie ▪ 6528 1774 ▪ Subway: Wangfujing ▪ Open 9am–9:30pm daily

A four-storied children's store on Beijing's main shopping street, with everything from carry-cots and strollers to local and imported toys. There's even an in-store play area.

5 Happy Valley

Xiaowuji Bei Lu, East 4th Ring Road ▪ 6738 3333 ▪ Open 9:30am–10pm daily ▪ Adm; children under 4 ft (1.2 m) free

This Disneyland-style park has 120 attractions over six themed regions. The park's aim is to keep both parents and children content by providing interactive education experiences. Thrill-seekers can enjoy no fewer than 40 rides, of which ten are "extreme," including a "Drop Tower" in which riders fall at 45 mph (72 km/h) in a terrifying simulated plunge to earth. There is also a shopping complex, and an IMAX cinema.

Thrilling ride at Happy Valley

Aquatic fun at the Water Cube

6 Water Cube
Olympic Park, 11 Tianchen Donglu, Chaoyang District ▪ 8437 0112 ▪ Subway: Olympic Sports Center ▪ Open 10am–10pm daily ▪ Adm; children under 4 ft (1.2 m) free

The 2008 Olympics Aquatics Center is now a water park. Water slides and giant inflatable rides will excite young fans, while the Bullet Bowl "plug hole" descent on a four-seater dinghy is a thrill for any age (see p44).

7 Blue Zoo Beijing
This small but beautifully done aquarium (see p89) has an enormous coral reef tank containing an array of visually exciting marine life, including eels, rays, and sharks. Tanks are set low enough for toddlers to peer into them. There's also a "marine tunnel", and shark-feeding sessions are held twice-daily.

8 Chaoyang Park
Subway: Liangmaqiao

There are plenty of rides and activities here, including zip-lining, for both children and adults. This is one of the few parks in the city where visitors walk, run, do yoga, kick balls, or lay down on real grass by the lake. Go early, take a picnic, and enjoy the day.

9 Kerry Center Adventure Zone
MAP H4 ▪ Kerry Center Hotel, 1 Guanghua Lu ▪ 8565 2490 ▪ Subway: Guomao ▪ Open 10am–9pm Mon–Fri, 9am–10pm Sat & Sun ▪ Adm

Parents and children can play together at this fun center with a three-story jungle gym, a tree house, vertical slides, and colorful cars. All areas are age specific, and weary adults can always take a break to relax at the nearby café.

Science and Technology Museum

10 Science and Technology Museum
This museum (see p101) has lots of hands-on exhibits for kids to pull, push, and even walk through. There is also an IMAX-style movie theater and an indoor play area in a separate building north of the main entrance.

📻10 Entertainment

A demonstration of martial arts by Shaolin monks

1 Martial Arts
The Shaolin monks from Songshan in Henan Province have gained an international reputation for their martial arts prowess. They perform regularly at the Li Yuan Theater *(see p53)*.

2 Acrobatics
China is renowned for the quality of its gymnasts, who perform breathtaking routines that showcase their unnerving flexibility. Displays of balance often involve props such as chairs, plates, and bicycles. Several Beijing theaters put on shows – for instance, the Chaoyang Theater; your hotel can help with reservations.

Acrobats on a bicycle

3 Cinema
The easy availability of streaming services means that most Beijingers watch movies at home. Publicly screened films are subject to censorship, but foreign cultural institutes host screenings of independent and classic films. For the latest movies, head to Wanda Cineplex.

4 Puppet Theater
Shadow-puppet theater is an art form that has been performed more or less unchanged in China since the 3rd century AD. Shows employ many of the story lines and musical styles of Beijing Opera, while the puppets can be quite elaborate and colorfully dressed. The best place to catch a performance is at the China Puppet Art Theater *(Anhua Xili, off Bei Sanhuan Lu)* in Chaoyang District.

5 Rock and Pop
Beijing has a thriving music scene supported by a host of small music bars and clubs *(see p59)*. Punk and metal thrive, and for those with a more eclectic taste, local folk rockers mix ethnic instrumentation with Western genres.

6 Sports
Soccer is big in Beijing. The local boys are Beijing Guo'an, who play in the Chinese Super League at the Workers' Stadium *(see p90)*. Book

tickets ahead or you might have to buy from a tout outside. Second in popularity is basketball. Aoshen, the top team, plays at the Beijing Guang'an Gymnasium *(Baiguang Lu; Map C6)*.

7 Traditional Music

If you can, attend a traditional Chinese orchestral performance. Sections of unfamiliar plucked string, bowed string, woodwind, and percussion instruments compete for attention in swirling arrangements. The main venues are the Forbidden City Concert Hall in Zhong Shan Park and the National Center for the Performing Arts *(see p70)*.

Performance of traditional music

8 Beijing Opera

With its incomprehensible plots, unfamiliar sounds, and performances lasting up to three hours, Beijing Opera is an acquired taste. Everyone should try it at least once *(see pp52–3)*.

9 Chinese Folk Dances

Performances showcasing China's 56 ethnic minorities, or nationalities, feature traditional costumes and dances. Some shows are truly outstanding, such as Yang Liping's famous peacock dance.

10 Theater

Beijing is home to several excellent theaters, where a few established troupes perform regularly. Canonical works such as Lao She's "Teahouse" are increasingly supplemented by big-budget Western musicals such as "Rent" and "Aladdin on Ice." See the English-language press for what's on.

TOP 10 PARKS

1 Bei Hai Park
Classic ornamental gardens *(see pp24–5)* with a large lake for boating.

2 Chaoyang Park
The largest afforested park *(see p49)* in Beijing.

3 Di Tan Park
Large green spaces and cypress trees, and the striking Altar of Earth *(see p83)*.

4 Xiang Shan Park
An hour's drive northwest of the center but worth it for thickly wooded slopes dotted with pavilions *(see p99)*.

5 Olympic Green
Subway: Forest Park
A 1,680-acre (680-hectare) green space, Beijing's largest park *(see p44)* is home to three Olympic venues.

6 Jing Shan Park
A hilly park *(see p71)* with a pavilion providing views of the roofscape of the Forbidden City to the south.

7 Long Tan Park
MAP G6 ▪ Subway: Tian Tan Dong Men
Lots of lakes, a kids' amusement park, and an enchanting water-screen show.

8 Ri Tan Park
One of Beijing's oldest parks, *(see p91)* featuring an altar for imperial sacrifice.

9 Temple of Heaven Park
This park *(see p16)* houses several historic structures and a vast expanse of well-tended gardens, including a rose garden.

10 Zhong Shan Park
Just outside the walls of the Forbidden City, Zhong Shan *(see p71)* offers a respite from the crowds.

Flying kites in a Beijing park

TOP 10 Beijing Opera

Preparing for the role of Monkey King

1 The Monkey King (Sun Wukong)

Clever, resourceful, and brave, the Monkey King is a favorite character in Beijing Opera. He has his origins in Chinese folklore, but was made famous by Wu Cheng'en's 16th-century classical novel *Journey to the West*.

2 Jing

There are four main role types in Beijing Opera: *sheng* (male), *dan* (female), *jing* (painted face), and *chou* (clown). *Jing* have stylized patterned, colored faces, and represent warriors, heroes, statesmen, adventurers, and demons. Not only do

Jing performers on stage

these characters have the most striking look of all the performers, they also usually have predominantly forceful personalities.

3 Dan

Dan are the female roles. *Laodan* are old ladies, *caidan* are female comedians, and *wudan* are martial artists. The most important category, *qingyi*, play respectable and decent ladies in elegant costumes.

4 Sheng

Sheng are divided into *laosheng*, who wear beards and represent old men, *xiaosheng* who are young men, and *wusheng*, who are acrobats.

5 Chou

The *chou* are the comic roles, characterized by white patches on their noses. Patches of different shape and size imply roles of different characters. It is the *chou* who keep the audience laughing.

The comic *chou* character

6 Mei Lanfang

The foremost male interpreter of the female role *(dan)* during Beijing Opera's heyday in the

1920s and 1930s was Mei Lanfang. All female roles were once played by male actors. However, this is no longer the case today.

 Colors
The colors of the performers' painted faces symbolize various qualities. Red, for example, stands for loyalty and courage, purple for solemnity and a sense of justice, and green for bravery and irascibility.

Women playing the erhu *violin*

8 Musical instruments
Despite the dramatic visual elements of Beijing Opera, the Chinese say that they go to "listen" to opera, not to see it. Typically six or seven musicians accompany the dramatics. The stringed instruments usually include the *erhu*, or Chinese two-stringed violin, while percussion includes clappers, gongs, and drums.

9 Acrobatics
Beijing Opera is a form of "total theater" with singing, speech, mime, and acrobatics that combine graceful gymnastics and martial arts movements. Training is notoriously hard. Costumes are designed to make the jumps seem more spectacular by billowing out as they spin.

10 Repertoire
The traditional repertoire includes more than 1,000 works, mostly based on popular tales. Modern productions aimed at tourists often include English-language displays of the text.

TOP 10 BEIJING OPERA VENUES

Show at Huguang Guild Hall

1 Huguang Guild Hall
MAP D5 ▪ 135 5252 7373 ▪ 3 Hufang Lu
One-hour highlights shows held on most days.

2 Chang'an Grand Theater
MAP G4 ▪ 7 Jianguo Men Nei Dajie ▪ 6510 1308
Regular two-hour performances of mostly complete operas.

3 Mei Lanfang Grand Theater
32 Ping'Anli Xi Dajie ▪ 5833 1217
A large steel-and-glass theater.

4 Tianqiao Performing Arts Center
MAP E6 ▪ Building 9, Tianqiao Nandajie, Xicheng District ▪ 400 635 3355 ▪ www.tartscenter.com
A massive arts venue specializing in ballet, musical theater and traditional opera.

5 National Center of Performing Arts
Beijing's temple to the arts offers large-scale performances (see p70).

6 Lao She Teahouse
MAP L6 ▪ 6303 6830 ▪ 3 Qian Men Xi Dajie ▪ www.laosheteahouse.com
Daily 90-minute variety shows.

7 Li Yuan Theater
MAP D6 ▪ 6301 6688 ▪ Qian Men Jianguo Hotel, 175 Yong'an Lu
Daily 80-minute highlights shows.

8 Mansion of Prince Gong
MAP D2 ▪ 8328 8149 ▪ 17 Qianhai Xi Jie
Summer performances only (see p27).

9 Forbidden City Concert Hall
MAP L4 ▪ 6559 8285 ▪ West Chang'an Avenue, Zhong Shan Park
Concert venue holding occasional opera performances.

10 Zheng Yi Ci Theater
MAP K6 ▪ 138 0106 7568 ▪ 220 Xiheyan Qian Men
Performances and 90-minute highlights shows held on selected days of the week.

TOP 10 Beijing Dishes

1 Thousand-year-old Eggs

These raw duck eggs are put into mud, chalk, and ammonia and left, not for 1,000 years, but several weeks. When retrieved, the yolk and white both appear darker in color. The eggs are either sprinkled with soy sauce and sesame oil, or served in rice porridge.

2 Hot Pot

Introduced to Beijing in the 13th century by the Mongols, hot pot is a much-loved staple. Hundreds of restaurants across the city sell this dish. Everybody sits around a large bubbling pot of broth dropping in their own shavings of meat, noodles, and vegetables to cook.

Whole roasted Beijing duck

Mongolian fire hot pot

3 Zha Jiang Mian

The name means "clanging dish noodles" – like hot pot, ingredients are added at the table to a central tureen of noodles, and the bowls are loudly clanged together as each dish goes in, hence the name.

4 Beijing Duck

This is arguably one of the best-known dishes in north Chinese cuisine. The duck, a local Beijing variety, is dried and brushed with a sweet marinade before being roasted over fragrant wood chips. It is carved by the chef and then eaten wrapped in pancakes with slivered scallions (spring onions) and cucumber.

5 La Mian

Watching a cook make *la mian* (hand-pulled noodles) is almost as enjoyable as eating them. First the dough is stretched and then swung like a skipping rope, so that it becomes plaited. The process is repeated several times, until the strands of dough are as thin as string.

6 Sweet and Sour Carp

Beijing cooking is heavily influenced by the cuisine of Shandong Province, generally regarded as the oldest and best in China. Sweet and sour carp is a quintessential Shandong dish traditionally made with fish from the Yellow River.

Zha jiang mian

7 Stir-fried Kidney Flowers

These are pork kidneys cut in a criss-cross fashion and stir-fried, during which they open out like "flowers." The kidneys are typically prepared with bamboo shoots, water chestnuts, and edible black fungus.

8 Drunken Empress Chicken

This dish is supposedly named for Yang Guifei, an imperial concubine who was overly fond of her alcohol. The dish is prepared using Chinese wine and is served cold.

Steamer stacked with various dumplings

9 Jiaozi

Traditional Beijing dumplings are filled with pork, *bai cai* (Chinese leaf), and ginger but, in fact, fillings are endless. You can find *jiaozi* at snack shops all over the city. They are also sold on the street, either steamed or fried on a giant hot plate over a brazier.

10 Lamb and Scallions

Scallions (spring onions) are a common Beijing ingredient and in this dish they are rapidly stir-fried along with sliced lamb, garlic, and a sweet-bean paste.

TOP 10 BEIJING STREET FOODS

1 Lu da gun'r
Literally "donkeys rolling in dirt": sweet red-bean paste in a rice dough dusted with peanut powder.

2 Jian bing
A Chinese crêpe often sold off the back of tricycles. It is a typical Beijing breakfast dish.

3 Shao bing
Hot bread roll sometimes filled with a fried egg and often sprinkled with aniseed for flavoring.

4 Tang chao lizi
Chestnuts, roasted in sugar and hot sand and served in a paper bag. A seasonal snack appearing in autumn.

5 Hong shu
A winter specialty, these are baked sweet potatoes, often heated in ovens made from oil drums.

6 Chuan'r
In any area with lots of bars and clubs you'll find street vendors selling *chuan'r* (kebabs). They cost just a few *yuan* per skewer.

7 Baozi
These delicious steamed dumplings are cooked in bamboo baskets. Typical fillings include pork, chicken, beef, or vegetables and tofu.

8 Rou bing
Cooked bread filled with finely chopped and spiced pork. A variant is *rou jiamo*, which is a bun packed with finely diced lamb.

9 You tiao
Deep-fried dough sticks, often dipped in warm congee (a rice porridge).

10 Tang hu lu
A kebab of candied hawthorn berries.

Skewered berries in a *tang hu lu*

Restaurants

Relaxed ambience at Mosto, an international bistro in Sanlitun

1 Mosto
Serving contemporary classics prepared by award-winning chef Daniel Urdaneta, Mosto *(see p93)* has plenty of fans thanks to its great wine list and immaculate service.

2 Georg
With a tasteful fine dining affair curated by the eponymous Danish silverware brand *(see p85)*, Georg has a minimalist design, and is located near a babbling brook. Sample the wine pairing and tasting menus.

Elegant dining at Georg

3 Din Tai Fung
24 Xinyuan Xili Middle Street
■ 6462 4502 ■ ¥¥
This place specializes in southern Chinese dishes, particularly the light, fresh flavors of Zhejiang and Jiangsu provinces. Try the *xialong bao*, juicy buns filled with pork or seafood prepared in a bamboo steamer, or the steamed dumplings with vegetables.

4 TRB Hutong
MAP M2 ■ 23 Shatan Beijie
■ 8400 2232 ■ Subway: Dong Si Shi Tiao ■ ¥¥¥
Located in a beautifully restored 600-year-old temple complex, this upmarket restaurant offers superb European cuisine. A second TRB branch is located near the Forbidden City, and promises an equally great dining experience *(see p73)*. Advance reservations are essential.

5 Toast at the Orchid
The Orchid gained fame as a stylish hotel at the end of a winding *hutong*, but the Middle Eastern-inspired mezze and tapas menu at its in-house restaurant *(see p85)* also has patrons raving. Come for dinner, stay for a drink, and soak up the atmosphere.

6 Lost Heaven
Located in the former US embassy, this restaurant *(see p79)* has plenty of authentic touches from the southwestern province of Yunnan. This is the most foreign-friendly of the Chinese cuisines, and it is famous for its local cheese.

7 Dali Courtyard

Beautifully lit by candles at night, this atmospheric courtyard venue (see p85) wins top marks for ambience, as well as for its excellent set menus made up of classic dishes from Yunnan province. It's a good idea to reserve a table.

8 Country Kitchen

A lively restaurant with an elegant decor (see p93), it offers a flavorful selection of northern Chinese dishes such as beef brisket, duck and black mushroom sauce, as well as Sichuan ones, like fiery chicken and prawns.

9 Mercante

Mercante (see p85) brings a rustic Mediterranean vibe to Beijing's hutongs, and is worth a visit for its authentic handmade pasta, homemade ricotta cheese, and organic beef. Good cooking takes time, but sip on some quality wines and enjoy the evening.

10 Cai Yi Xuan

With its award-winning cuisine, Cai Yi Xuan (see p93) offers a fine dining experience. Especially popular are their artistically presented Cantonese dishes such as sea cucumber, abalone, and seasonal hairy crab.

Refined table setting at Cai Yi Xuan

TOP 10 CHEAP EATS

Steamed dumplings

1 Mr Shi's Dumplings
MAP E1 ▪ 88 Baochao Hutong, Gulou Donglu
MSG-free dumplings and local dishes served by English-speaking staff.

2 Ling Er Jiu Noodles
Xingfucun Zhong Lu, Sanlitun
Some of the best noodles in Beijing are served here.

3 Pingwa Sanbao
10A Xiangjunzhuang Lu
Offers hand-pulled noodles and chuan'r (kebabs).

4 Green Bites Dumpling Bar
Kirin Place lobby, 11 Fu'an Xi Lu
Socially responsible dumplings, with eco-friendly carry-out boxes.

5 Mama de Weidao
6–110 Zhongguo Hong Jie Building, 2 Gongti Dong Lu
Home-style northern cuisine.

6 The Southern Fish
49 Gongmenkou Toutiao
The impossibly spicy Hunan food here attracts plenty of locals; reserve ahead.

7 Nice Rice
23 Dongsiertiao, Dongcheng
Hunan cuisine in modern surrounds; try stir-fried tofu and fiery beef dishes.

8 Zhang Mama
76 Jiaodoukou Nan Dajie
This is the place for hot Sichuan snacks; even the scrambled eggs are packed with chili.

9 Yun Er Small Town
84 Beiluoguxiang
Yunnan fare on a rooftop terrace; try the potatoes cooked with tea leaves.

10 Tiger Mama
Building 38, Sanlitun Xijie
Macanese shop offering wet or dry noodles, fish balls, and beef offal.

For a key to restaurant price ranges see p73

🔟 Bars and Pubs

Ingredients for cocktails at Manhattan-style bar Janes and Hooch

1 Janes and Hooch
MAP H2 ▪ Courtyard 4, Gongti Bei Lu ▪ 6503 2757 ▪ Subway: Tuanjiehu
Cocktails, bourbons, and ales are served at this split-level speakeasy bar and lounge to the accompaniment of smooth jazz and blues music.

2 Botany Bar
MAP H2 ▪ 1209 Unit 2, Yonglee Plaza, Gongti Bei Lu ▪ 6463 6091
Swanky yet homey apartment bar with work-of-art cocktails such as Amortentia, infused with rosemary sprigs and toasted sesame seeds.

3 La Social
MAP H2 ▪ 3rd Floor, Nali Patio, 81 Sanlitun Lu ▪ 5208 6030
This is a Columbian bar with serious food options, including *arepas* (corn

Fried *arepas* at La Social

flatbreads with varied fillings), and excellent cocktails. The eclectic decor includes a picture of Jesus framed by yellow bulbs, velvet lampshades, and neon busts of Mao. It is closed on Sundays.

Pina colada cocktail

4 Mai
This smartly designed cocktail bar, Mai *(see p84)*, has outdoor seating in a narrow courtyard, plus a giant silver sofa and bar chairs inside. It draws a cool *hutong* crowd, especially at weekends.

5 Migas
MAP H2 ▪ 6/F Nali Patio, 81 Sanlitun Bei Lu ▪ 5208 6061 ▪ Subway: Tuanjiehu
This chic Spanish restaurant and rooftop terrace bar is always packed with a hip cocktail-drinking crowd that comes here for the DJs and great alfresco views. Try the chargrilled octopus.

6 Hidden House
MAP H2 ▪ 39 Xin Dong Lu, Chaoyang District ▪ 8418 5718
The cozy alcoves at this utterly charming speakeasy are perfect for quiet conversation and the cocktails are new takes on old favorites.

(7) Slow Boat Brewery
MAP H3 ■ 6 Sanlitun Nan Lu
■ 6592 5388 ■ Subway: Tuanjiehu

A seasonally updated selection
of delicious beers and award-
winning burgers are served at
this smart but laid-back bar,
run by two American expats.

Craft beers at Slow Boat Brewery

(8) Amilal
48 Shoubi Hutong,
Dongcheng District ■ 8404 1416

This Mongolian-owned whiskey bar
in a tiny *hutong* has it all – a mish-
mash of comfortable furniture,
random cultural artifacts, tiny
tables, hushed conversation,
and a number of roaming cats.

(9) Centro
MAP H4 ■ Kerry Center
Hotel, 1 Guanghua Lu ■ 8565 2398
■ Subway: Guomao

Set in the lobby of one of the city's
swankiest hotels, Centro boasts live
music and the last word in cocktails.

Tables on the deck terrace at Mesh

(10) Mesh
MAP H2 ■ B1, The Opposite
House, 11 Sanlitun Bei Lu ■ 6410
5220 ■ Subway: Tuanjiehu

Ultra-trendy lounge bar Mesh
features a cool outdoor deck terrace
and bamboo garden. It's a popular
spot for after-work cocktails and
evening drinks on weekends.

TOP 10 MUSIC BARS

1 Dusk Dawn Club
14 Shanlao Hutong, Dongcheng
District ■ 6407 8969
Courtyard venue with trees growing
through tables and regular live shows.

2 School Live Bar
53 Wudaoying Hutong, Dongcheng
District ■ 6402 8881
This *hutong* venue is one of the city's
best music spots.

3 Yugong Yishan
3-2 Zhangzizhong Lu ■ 6404 2711
The city's most satisfying music venue,
with an eclectic booking policy.

4 Blue Note
MAP M6 ■ 23 Qian Men Dong Dajie
■ 170 0000 0288
The jazz club's first branch in China.

5 Dada
MAP E2 ■ 183 1108 0818 ■ 206
Gulou Dong Dajie
Super-hip DJ lounge and mini club
import from Shanghai.

6 Hot Cat Club
MAP F1 ■ 6400 7868 ■ 46 Fangjia
Hutong
This compact pub is the mainstay
of Beijing's live Indie music scene.

7 Modernista
A 1920s-themed jazz and piano bar
(see p84) that also serves Spanish tapas.

8 Temple Bar
MAP E2 ■ 206 Gulou Dong Dajie
■ 131 6107 0713
This institution has live shows, a
wide drink selection and late-night
pub food.

9 East Shore Live Jazz Cafe
A classic pure jazz venue *(see p84)* with
terrific views over Hou Hai.

10 Jianghu Bar
MAP E2 ■ 7 Dongmianhua Hutong,
Jiaodaokou Nan Dajie ■ 6401 5269
Cozy courtyard bar hosting jam sessions.

Jianghu Bar's rustic interior

TOP10 Markets and Shops

Pearls at Hong Qiao Market

1 Hong Qiao Market

Hong Qiao (see p78) is best known for pearls (hence its alternative name, the "Pearl Market"), with a huge range of freshwater and seawater ones available on the third floor. The floors below are a tight compress of clothing, shoes, electronics, and more. The basement is a pungent, but fascinating, market for fish, frogs, and snakes.

2 Oriental Plaza

A large mall (see p72) that stretches a whole city block and features several levels of top-end retailers including Paul Smith, Swarovski, Sisley, Max Mara, and Apple. There is also a Watsons drugstore, a big CD and DVD store, and an excellent food court.

3 Chongwenmen Market

MAP G6 ■ Guangqumenwai Dajie, Chaoyang District ■ Subway: Guangqumennei ■ 6701 8014 ■ Open 8am–9pm daily
Located to the east of the Temple of Heaven, this is one of the oldest food markets in the city and offers an authentic Chinese experience. It is also surprisingly clean.

4 Plastered T-Shirts

MAP E2 ■ 61 Nan Luogu Xiang, Dongcheng District ■ 6406 4872 ■ Open 9:30am–11pm daily
A great place for gifts, Plastered offers quirky Beijing style in the form of T-shirts and tote bags. Founder Dominic Johnson Hill works with Chinese designers, and everything is manufactured in the capital. There is another shop in the 798 Art District.

5 Three Stone Kite Shop

MAP K1 ■ 25A Di'an Men Xi Dajie, Xicheng District ■ 8404 4505 ■ Open 9am–9pm daily ■ www.cnkites.com
Owner and craftsman, Liu Bin, comes from a long line of kite makers, some of whom once served the royal family. His kites are true works of art. Sturdy enough for Beijing breezes, they also make for exquisite, lightweight gifts. The shop runs kite-making classes, too.

Taikoo Li Sanlitun shopping center

8 Cathay Bookshop (Zhongguo Shudian)
Liulichang Xi Jie ▪ 6317 3805
▪ Open 9am–5pm daily

A bookstore with a vast selection of modern Chinese art books, as well as classic second-hand, vintage, and antique collections.

9 Beijing Postcards
97 Yangmeizhuxiejie ▪ 156 1145 3992 ▪ www.bjpostcards.com

This fascinating shop sells historic Beijing postcards, maps, calendars, and prints from the 1870s–1940s, all purchased at auction or from descendants of missionaries. See the website for information on their lectures and historical walking tours.

6 Taikoo Li Sanlitun
This hip shopping, dining, and entertainment center *(see p92)* in Sanlitun has numerous colored glass buildings housing over 200 stores, including global brand flagships such as the Apple Store and Nike, plus some of downtown Beijing's best bars and cafés.

7 Panjiayuan Antique Market
As much a tourist attraction as a shopping experience, Panjiayuan *(see p78)* is home to around 3,000 dealers peddling everything from broken bicycles to family heirlooms. Come here for Mao memorabilia, a Qing-dynasty vase, or Tintin comics in Chinese. Panjiayuan Market is at its busiest and best on weekends. Serious collectors swoop at dawn, but it's fun any time of the day.

Colorful fabrics at the Silk Market

10 Silk Market
Properly known as Xiushui, this market *(see p92)* is reportedly one the city's most popular tourist attractions, after the Forbidden City and the Great Wall. The bargains are not what they used to be, but some 100,000 shoppers a day still visit to snap up famous brand goods.

Antiques on display at Panjiayuan

TOP 10 Beijing for Free

1 Museums

Many of Beijing's big national museums – including the Natural History Museum (see p77), the National Museum of China (see p70), and the National Art Museum of China (see p70) – offer free entry, although you may be asked to pay a small fee for an optional guide. The Capital Museum (see p94) is free but requires you to make an online reservation before you visit.

2 Former Residence of Lao She

MAP M3 ▪ 19 Fengfu Lane, Dengshikou Xije, Dongcheng District ▪ 6514 2612 ▪ Subway: Fuchengmen ▪ Open 9am–4pm Tue–Sun

This well-preserved courtyard home with a memorial honors Beijing personality and Chinese luminary Lao She, author of such literary classics as *Teahouse* and *Rickshaw Boy*.

3 Beijing University Campus

5 Yiheyuan Road, Haidian District ▪ 0506 5075 ▪ Subway: Peking University (East Gate)

Known locally as PKU (Peking University), Beijing University is a sprawling campus, complete with a willow-lined lake. It also features Haidian's best theater venue.

4 Southern Moat and Central Axis

MAP E6 (Southern Moat) ▪ Access to Southern Moat via Yongdingmen Gate ▪ Access to Central Axis via Yonghe Gong Park

Beijing's once-extensive moat network has been diminished by centuries of war, structural changes, and a drying climate. Still, walking the footpath along the palace's Southern Moat is a peaceful trip back to the old city.

5 Panjiayuan Antique Market

Once called the "dirt market," when farmers used to literally unearth treasures and bring them here to sell, today Panjiayuan (see p78) is where you'll find all sorts of antiques, from carved furniture to propaganda art and Qing-dynasty pottery.

Statuary at Panjiayuan Antique Market

6 The Chinese Museum of Women and Children

MAP F4 ▪ 23 Jianguomennei Dajie ▪ 6526 9456 ▪ Subway: Dongdan ▪ Open 9am–5pm Tue–Sun

Housed in a wonderfully sinuous modern building, this museum examines how the role of women has changed through history, as well as their clothing and art. The children's section isn't quite as interesting, but has plenty of activities for kids.

Leafy grounds at Beijing University Campus

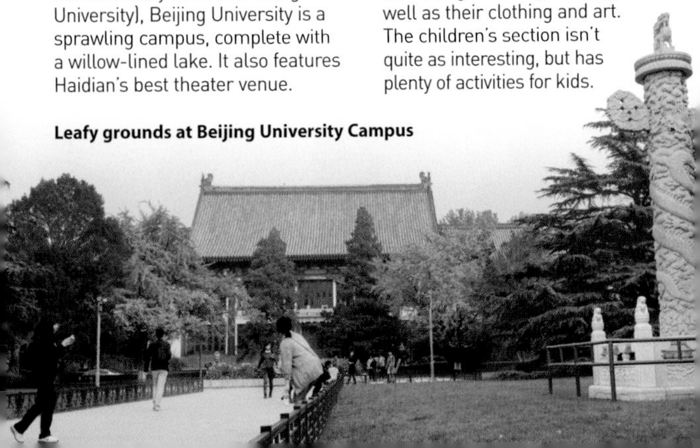

Charming Beijing *hutong*

 Hutongs
Although they're disappearing fast due to redevelopment, *Hutongs*, or traditional lanes, are where you'll find Beijing's old-world charm. Try Nanluoguxiang and Beiluoguxiang *hutongs*, near Gulou; Fangjia and Wudaoying *hutongs*, across from the Lama Temple; and Dashilan *hutong* in the Qian Men area.

8 Street Dancing
The so-called "dancing grannies" are senior citizens who meet in public squares for social-izing and getting light exercise through activities such as fan and ballroom dancing, drumming, or low-key aerobics. This is one of Beijing's more charming features.

9 Yishu 8
MAP M2 ▪ 20 Dong Huangchengen Bei Jie, Dongcheng District ▪ 6581 9058 ▪ Subway: Dongsi, Nanluoguxiang ▪ Open 11am–6:30pm Mon–Sat
Housed in the old Sino-French University, Yishu 8 hosts regular exhibitions featuring cross-cultural collaborations of Chinese and French artists. Each room has its own style, and the leafy courtyard offers welcome respite from the city.

10 Maliandao (Tea Street)
There's little charm about Maliandao (see p78), which is basically a tea mall for wholesalers. However, here you can see, smell, and learn everything you ever wanted to know about tea. There's an impressive range of flower types, and you can enjoy unlimited free samples.

(see p78)

TOP 10 BUDGET TIPS

1 Tickets
Research museums and other sights online to decide which to visit. For some sights, you can buy an all-access pass or a single-zone pass.

2 Connections
Every café has free Wi-Fi, and WeChat offers free international texts, voice messages, and phone calls.

3 Airport Transit
Upon disembarking, catch the airport express (¥25), then transfer to a bus or subway at Dong Zhi Men.

4 Street Food
Eating delicious *chuan'r* (roasted kebabs) or *malatang* (boiled kebabs) paired with a ¥2 local beer will be a highlight of your stay in Beijing.

5 Museums
On Wednesdays, 13 museums offer free admission to the first 200 visitors.

6 Public Spectacle
Dancing or doing tai chi with the locals costs nothing, and the experience will create a priceless memory.

7 Self-Restraint
Markets are exercises in bargaining, but the best deals come before closing time, so be sure to pace yourself.

8 Dorm Life
Opt for a hostel over a hotel; beds are cheap, and the hostel locations are among the best in the city.

9 Two-Wheelers
Travel like a local and rent a bicycle, or register for public bicycles on the street. Cycle on a quiet side street first.

10 Public Transport
Forget taxis; the Beijing subway costs only ¥6. Beijing IC offer a 60 per cent discount on buses.

Rack of public bicycles

🔟 Festivals and Events

Fireworks and traditional dances heralding Chinese New Year

1 Chinese New Year
Three days from the 1st day of the 1st moon, usually late Jan or early Feb

Also known as Spring Festival, Beijing's favorite holiday sees fireworks let off night and day across the city, plus temple fairs with stilt-walkers, acrobats, and fortune-tellers. Families make *jiaozi* (dumplings) together and exchange gifts, then the adults watch the annual Spring Festival Gala on television.

2 Lantern Festival
The 15th day of the lunar calendar (end of Feb)

This festival marks the end of the 15-day Spring Festival celebrations. Lanterns bearing auspicious characters or in the shape of animals are hung everywhere. It is also a time for eating the sticky rice balls known as *yuanxiao*.

Decorative Lantern

3 Tomb-Sweeping Festival (Qing Ming)
Apr 5, but Apr 4 in leap years

On this public holiday, Chinese families visit their ancestors' graves to tidy them up, make offerings of snacks and alcohol, and burn incense and paper money.

4 International Labor Day
May 1

Labor Day is celebrated with a three-day holiday, which marks the start of the domestic travel season. Shops, offices, and other businesses close for the entire holiday, and often for a whole week. Don't plan on doing any out-of-town travel during this time.

5 Dragon Boat Festival (Duanwu Jie)
The 5th day of the 5th lunar month (early Jun)

This festival remembers the honest official, Qu Yuan, who drowned himself about 2,500 years ago, after banishment from the court of the Duke of Chu. Citizens threw rice cakes into the water to distract the fish from nibbling on his body, hence the wholesale consumption of these delicacies on this date. Drums thunder as dragon-headed craft compete for top honors.

Dragon Boat Festival competition

Chinese Valentine's Day
The 7th day of the 7th lunar month (usually Aug)

This festival celebrates the forbidden love between a mortal and a goddess. Couples exchange gifts, and single women take fruit or flowers to a temple and pray for love.

Mid-Autumn Festival
The 15th day of the 8th lunar month (usually Sep)

Also known as the Harvest or Moon Festival, this is traditionally a time for family reunions and for giving boxes of sweet and savory mooncakes *(yuebing)*.

National Day
Oct 1

On the anniversary of the foundation of the People's Republic, crowds turn out to watch military parades in Tian'an Men Square, which is colored red by a sea of waving flags.

National Day on Tian'an Men Square

 Hairy Crab Season
Oct to early Dec

This is a two-month celebration of China's favorite winter delicacy, hairy crabs, which are in season during the ninth and tenth months of the Chinese lunar calendar. Prized for their creamy meat, these are served in packed restaurants across the city.

 Christmas Day
Dec 25

Not a traditional Chinese holiday but the festivities have been adopted via Hong Kong, which means that the focus is on squarely consumerism.

TOP 10 CULTURAL EVENTS

1 Temple Fairs
Jan/Feb
Colorful street fairs outside the city's large temples during Chinese New Year.

2 Longqing Gorge Ice and Snow Festival
MAP G5 ▪ Longqing Gorge ▪ Jan & Feb
Showcases giant ice and snow sculptures illuminated by pretty colored lights in a rural setting 25 miles (40 km) northwest of Beijing (see p105).

3 Surge
Spring and autumn
Emerging artists' exhibitions take place at the Red Gate Gallery (see p30).

4 Beijing International Film Festival
Various venues ▪ Apr
This is China's largest film festival.

5 Beijing Music Festival (BMF)
Oct
Featuring the biggest names in music.

6 Art Beijing
National Agricultural Exhibition Center ▪ May
Contemporary art fair with exhibitors from around the globe.

7 Croisements Festival
May–Jun
Festival blending French and Chinese culture, often on the same stage.

8 NLGX Performing Arts Festival
Jun–Aug
International players perform in venues in Nan Luogu Xiang (see p81).

9 Beijing Dance Festival
Jul
Established modern dance companies perform alongside emerging talent.

10 Meet in Beijing Festival
Apr–Jun
A festival of theater, dance, and music by groups from several continents.

Opera, Meet in Beijing Festival

Beijing
Area by Area

High-rises reflected on the water in
Beijing's Central Business District

TOP 10 Tian'an Men Square and the Forbidden City Area

The geographical, spiritual, and historical heart of Beijing, Tian'an Men Square and the Forbidden City together represent a yin and yang arrangement; one is a vast, empty public space, the other is an even larger walled enclosure. One represents modern China, while the other is a silent repository of ancient imperial glories. It is worth setting aside a whole day for each. Afterward, wander around the corner for a look at the National Center for the Performing Arts and a glimpse of the China of the future.

Vase at the National Museum of China

1 Tian'an Men Square

Although now synonymous with Beijing, until relatively recently there was no Tian'an Men Square (see pp18–19). For centuries this was just a main thoroughfare leading to the Gate of Heavenly Peace (Tian'an Men). Cleared in the first half of the 20th century, the area quadrupled in size in 1959, supposedly allowing for up to one million people to gather. Many of the buildings on the square were erected at this time.

The vast Great Hall of the People

2 Great Hall of the People

MAP L5 ■ West side of Tian'an Men Square ■ 6309 6156 ■ Subway: Tian'an Men West ■ Opening hours vary ■ Adm

This is the parliament building, home of China's legislative body, the National People's Congress. Tours visit the banquet room and the 10,000-seat auditorium, with its ceiling inset with a massive red star. The building is closed to the public when the Congress is in session.

1 Top 10 Sights
see pp68–71

1 Restaurants
see p73

1 Shops and Venues
see p72

3 Forbidden City

The Forbidden City is Beijing's top "must-see" sight *(see pp12–15)*. A seemingly endless collection of pavilions, gates, courts, and gardens, this majestic complex encompasses five centuries of colorful – and occasionally lurid – imperial history. Until the mid-1900s, only members of the imperial court were allowed inside – hence the name. Trying to see everything in one go will bring on a severe case of Ming fatigue, and it is highly recommended that you tackle this wonderful palace over at least two separate visits.

Bronze lion at the Forbidden City

TIAN'AN MEN SQUARE AND THE FORBIDDEN CITY AREA

④ Imperial City Art Museum

MAP M5 ■ 9 Changpu Heyan
■ 8511 5114 ■ Subway: Tian'an Men
East ■ Open 10am–4pm Tue–Sun
■ Adm ■ Audio tour available for a fee

Much of Beijing's Imperial City was
destroyed under the Communists. A
model in this museum shows just
how much has been lost, including
the wall that once encircled the city
and many temples. There are also
collections of armor and ceramics.

Fountain at Wangfujing Dajie

⑤ Wangfujing Dajie

MAP N4 ■ Subway: Wangfujing

One of downtown Beijing's most
famous shopping precincts,
Wangfujing Dajie is filled with
department stores, restaurants,
and malls (see p72), as well as
several bookshops and stores selling
silk, tea, and shoes. To the north is
St. Joseph's, one of the city's most
important churches (see p42).

⑥ National Art Museum of China

MAP M2 ■ 1 Wusi Dajie ■ 8403
3500 ■ Subway: Dong Si Shi Tiao
■ Open 9am–5pm Tue–Sun
■ Audio guides available for a fee
■ www.namoc.org

China's largest art gallery was one
of ten key buildings erected in 1959
to celebrate the tenth anniversary

THE CULT OF MAO

Mao Zedong was an ideologue whose
impatience at the pace of reform often
brought disaster, yet skillful maneuvering
by the Party meant that he remained a
heroic figure. Mao's status diminished in
the years after his death as his influence
was overshadowed by the political and
economic reforms carried out by Deng
Xiaoping and other leaders.

of the founding of the People's
Republic. Its 14 halls, spread
over three floors, host a constant
rotation of temporary exhibitions
of Chinese and international art.

⑦ National Museum of China

MAP M5 ■ East side of Tian'an Men
Square ■ 6511 6400 ■ Subway:
Tian'an Men East ■ Open 9am–5pm
Tue–Sun ■ www.chnmuseum.cn

Combining the original Museum of
Chinese History and the Museum
of the Revolution, this huge space
offers an unsurpassed collection of
Chinese artworks and other historical,
archaeological, and cultural objects.
There are also models, documents,
and photographs connected with the
history of the Chinese Communist
Party – for political enthusiasts
only. The museum also hosts
temporary exhibitions.

⑧ National Center for the Performing Arts

MAP K5 ■ 2 West Chang An Jie
■ 6655 0000 ■ Subway: Tian'an Men
West ■ www.chncpa.org

This modern opera house, a major
landmark on Beijing's skyline, hosts a
year-round program of opera, theater,
and concerts. Designed by French
architect Paul Andreu, it is built of

**National Center for the
Performing Arts**

glass and titanium and takes the form of a giant parabolic dome – earning it the nickname "The Egg." Entrance is through an underwater tunnel.

9 Jing Shan Park
MAP L2 ▪ 1 Wenjin Jie ▪ 6404 4071 ▪ Subway: Shichahai ▪ Bus: 5, 111, 124 ▪ Open 6am–9pm daily (Nov–Mar: 6:30am–8pm daily) ▪ Adm

Jing Shan (Coal Hill) lies north of the Forbidden City. The hill, created from the earth that was excavated while building the moat around the palace complex, was meant to protect the emperor and his court from malign northern influences, which brought death and destruction according to *feng shui*. The park is dotted with pavilions and halls, but the highlight is the view over the Forbidden City from the hilltop Wancheng Pavilion.

View from the hill of Jing Shan Park

10 Zhong Shan Park
MAP L4 ▪ 6605 5431 ▪ Subway: Tian'an Men West ▪ Open 6am–9pm daily ▪ Adm

Northwest of the Tian'an Men, Zong Shan (also known as Sun Yat Sen Park), the oldest and largest park in the city, offers respite from the crowds thronging the nearby sights. It was once part of the grounds of a temple, and the square Altar of Earth and Harvests remains. Located here is the Forbidden City Concert Hall, Beijing's premier venue for classical music.

A DAY AROUND TIAN'AN MEN SQUARE AND WANGFUJING DAJIE

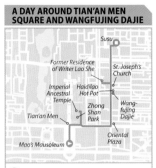

▶ MORNING

Arrive early to beat the crowds at **Mao's Mausoleum** *(see p19)* and shuffle through for the permitted few minutes in the presence of the Great Helmsman. The Forbidden City can be saved for another day, but climb the **Tian'an Men** *(see p18)* for the views from the gallery. From the gate, walk east along the Imperial City wall, soon arriving at an entrance overlooked by most visitors: this leads to the Imperial Ancestral Temple, an ancient place of worship. Take a walk through **Zhong Shan Park** and stop by the box office to check about concert tickets before heading east to **Wangfujing Dajie** and the **Oriental Plaza** mall *(see p60)*. Browse Beijing's first ritzy shopping district, then hit **Haidilao Hot Pot** *(see p73)* for lunch.

AFTERNOON

Wander up **Wangfujing Dajie**, making sure to look in the chopstick and teas shops. At No. 74 is the attractive **St. Joseph's Church** *(see p42)*, which is well worth a look. Immediately before the church is a crossroads: head away from the church along Deng Shi Kou Jie looking for signs for Fengfu Hutong on your right. Here is the **Former Residence of Writer Lao She** *(see p62)*, offering a glimpse into a way of life fast disappearing in Beijing. Keep heading north to **Susu** *(see p73)*, for a Vietnamese dinner in a converted courtyard.

See map on pp68–9

Shops and Venues

(1) Oriental Plaza
MAP N5 ■ 1 Dong Chang'an Jie
Several floors of high-end, big-name international retailers, from Apple and Sony to designers such as Armani and Paul Smith. Don't expect to find any bargains.

(2) Foreign Languages Bookstore
MAP N4 ■ 235 Wangfujing Dajie
Most of the first floor here is devoted to English-language fiction and non-fiction works and the staff are reliably surly.

(3) Ten Fu's Tea
MAP N4 ■ 88 Wangfujing Dajie
■ www.tenfu.com
Tea from all over China is sold loose or in beautiful presentation boxes at this lovely shop. Staff will even brew small cups for sampling.

(4) APM
MAP N4
■ 138 Wangfujing Dajie
This shopping mall full of mid-range clothes shops also has a multiscreen cinema as well as plenty of restaurants on the top floor.

(5) Gongmei Building
MAP N4
■ 200 Wangfujing Dajie
A vast, multistory emporium of all kinds of handicrafts, from cloisonné vases and jade to wood carvings, lacquer ware, and silks.

(6) Mao's Mausoleum
MAP L5 ■ Tian'an Men Square
■ Subway: Qian Men ■ Open 8:30–11:30am Mon–Sat, 2–4pm Mon, Wed & Fri
The mausoleum gift shop is the best source of Mao badges, posters, and shoulder bags.

(7) Forbidden City Concert Hall
MAP L4 ■ West Chang'an Avenue, Zhong Shan Park ■ 6559 8285
This venue draws the best musicians in town. In summer, the Gateway to Music Festival sees big names and traditional music concerts (see p53).

(8) Capital Theater
MAP N4 ■ 22 Wangfujing Dajie
■ 6512 1598
The city's smartest theater plays classic Chinese dramas, plus the occasional foreign Shakespeare show, to captivated audiences.

(9) Hao Yuan Market
MAP N4 ■ Off Wangfujing Dajie
A small street market just off Wangfujing, Hao Yuan is crammed with stalls selling knick-knacks, local handicrafts, and curios.

(10) Intime Lotte
MAP N4 ■ 88 Wangfujing Dajie
This high-end mall is jointly owned by the Korean department giant Lotte and the Chinese Intime group. It also hosts cultural events and exhibitions.

Intime Lotte

Restaurants

1 Susu
MAP M2 = 10 Qiangliang Xixiang, off Qianliang Hutong = 8400 2699 = ¥¥

Susu serves light Vietnamese fare, including spring rolls. The English-speaking staff can turn meat dishes into vegetarian options. Book ahead.

2 Dong Lai Shun
MAP N4 = 198 Wangfujing Dajie = 6513 9661 = ¥¥

An old name well-known for Mongolian-style hot pots. Get plates of sliced meat and vegetables to cook your own meal in a copper-funneled pot.

Oriental Plaza Food Court

3 Oriental Plaza Food Court
MAP N4 = Corner of Dong Chang'an Jie and Wangfujing Dajie = ¥

The basement of this upscale shopping mall has a Southeast Asian-style food court offering everything from good Chinese street food to sushi.

4 Made In China
MAP N5 = Grand Hyatt, 1 Dong Chang'an Jie = 6510 9608 = ¥¥¥

A classy venture with stunning design and even better food.

5 Jing
MAP N4 = The Peninsula Beijing Hotel, 8 Jinyu Hutong = 8516 2888 (ext 6758) = ¥¥¥

Enjoy an outstanding Asian-flavored French menu in refined surrounds.

PRICE CATEGORIES

For the equivalent of a meal for two made up of a range of dishes, served with two glasses of wine, and including service.

¥ under ¥250   ¥¥ ¥250–¥500
¥¥¥ over ¥500

6 TRB Forbidden City
95 Donghuamen Dajie, Dongcheng District = 6401 6676 = ¥¥¥

One of Beijing's top restaurants shows its more casual side, but its pedigree shines through. Choose from around 20 selections to customize your three to five courses. Another TRB branch is located at Shatan Beijie, Dongcheng District (see p56).

7 Haidilao Hot Pot
MAP N4 = 8th Floor, Tianyingtai Department Store, 88 Wangfujing Dajie = 5762 0153 = ¥¥

Try their delicious hotpot and friendly service. Get your shoes shined, or have a manicure while you wait.

8 Quanjude
MAP N5 = 9 Shuai Fu Yuan Hutong, Wangfujing Dajie = 6525 3310 = ¥¥

Beijing's famous duck restaurant has several branches but this is definitely the most convenient, just a short walk from southern Wangfujing.

9 Tianjin Bai Jiaoyuan
12 Xinwenhua Jie, Xicheng District = 6605 9371 = ¥

Loosely translated as "100 dumplings," and hailing from the neighboring city of Tianjin, this spot is known for its incredible variety of fillings and dumpling skin colors.

10 Huang Ting
MAP N4 = The Peninsula Beijing Hotel, 8 Jinyu Hutong = 8516 2888 (ext 6757) = ¥¥

Enjoy Cantonese cuisine amid splendid antique furniture in the basement of a five-star hotel.

See map on pp68–9

TOP 10 South of Tian'an Men Square

The Qian Men (Front Gate) at the southern end of Tian'an Men Square was once part of the inner walls that divided the imperial quarters from the "Chinese city," where the massed populace lived. Walking south from the gate you are plunged into a network of lively *hutongs* (alleys), the remnants of the old quarter. Continuing south down Qian Men Dajie brings you to the western perimeter of the grounds of the Temple of Heaven, one of Beijing's most evocative sights.

Incense burner at Fayuan Temple

1 Fayuan Temple

MAP C6 ■ 7 Fayuan Si Qian Jie ■ 6353 4171 ■ Subway: Caishikou, then a 10-minute walk ■ Open 8:30am–3:30pm daily ■ Adm

Dating from AD 696, this is most likely the oldest temple in Beijing. Near the gate, the incense burner is flanked by the Drum and Bell Towers. Beyond, the Hall of the Heavenly Kings is guarded by a pair of bronze lions. A hall contains a large statue of Buddha.

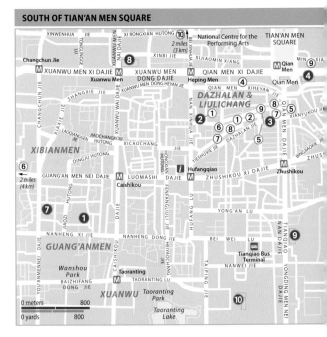

SOUTH OF TIAN'AN MEN SQUARE

Colorful building in Liulichang

2 Liulichang
MAP D5 ■ Subway: Heping Men

Head west from the bustle of Qian Men and Dazhalan into a more peaceful *hutong* district. Historically a gathering spot for writers, artists, and musicians, Liulichang takes its name from the glazed tile factory once located here. The streets are lined with shops selling Chinese paintings, musical instruments, porcelain, and calligraphy – look out for the giant ink brushes hanging in the windows. During Chinese New Year, Liulichang is home to one of Beijing's most colorful Temple Fairs.

3 Qian Men and Dazhalan
MAP D5–E5 ■ Subway: Qian Men

A historical royal street as well as a traditional shopping area, Qian Men Dajie has been redeveloped into a period-themed shopping boulevard replete with a faux-1920s tram and birdcage-like streetlamps. Running east and west off the northern end of Qian Men is Dazhalan Jie, or Dashilan, an old *hutong* area that can be explored on foot or by rickshaw. It is full of Qing-era specialty shops selling pickles, tea, silks, as well as traditional Chinese medicine.

4 Beijing Planning Exhibition Hall
MAP L6 ■ 20 Qian Men Dong Dajie ■ 6701 7074 ■ Subway: Qian Men ■ Open 9am–5pm Tue–Sun ■ www.bjghzl.com.cn

On display at this four-floor museum are dreams of the architecture and urban landscape of Beijing to be. These are dramatically represented through film and interactive exhibits, plus a vast model that covers most of the third floor. An interesting section is dedicated to Beijing's urban makeover for the 2008 Olympics.

Beijing Planning Exhibition Hall

⑤ Legation Quarter
MAP M5 ▪ Subway: Qian Men

At the end of the Second Opium War, in 1860, foreign delegations were permitted to take up residence in a quarter southeast of the Forbidden City. On Dong Jiao Min Xiang and the surrounding streets, the first modern foreign buildings in Beijing took root. The embassies have long since left, and new occupants have moved in. The former American legation, for instance, is now a bar, restaurant, and lifestyle complex. Also here are the former City Bank of New York, now the Beijing Police Museum (see p40), and St. Michael's Church (see p43).

THE BOXERS

The Boxers, a band of xenophobic rebels from north China who rose up to rid China of the "foreign devils," drew from superstitious rituals that they believed made them invulnerable. Supported by the Empress Dowager Cixi (see p29), the rebels laid waste to Beijing's Legation Quarter in 1900 while besieging the district's foreign population. The siege was eventually broken by an eight-power allied force.

⑥ Temple of Heaven
The name refers to a vast complex that encompasses a large, marble sacrificial altar, the iconic three-story Hall of Prayer for Good Harvests, the smaller Imperial Vault of Heaven, and many ancillary buildings, all set in a landscaped park. Allow at least a half-day to take in everything (see pp16–17).

Ornate hall in the Temple of Heaven

Looking inside Niu Jie Mosque

⑦ Niu Jie Mosque
MAP C6 ▪ 88 Niu Jie ▪ 6353 2564 ▪ Subway: Guanganmennei, then walk ▪ Open 8am–sunset daily ▪ Adm

Beijing's oldest and largest mosque dates back to the 10th century. It's an attractive building with Islamic motifs and Arabic verses decorating its halls. Astronomical observations were made from the tower-like Wangyue Lou. The lush courtyard is an idyllic escape from the city streets. Visitors should dress conservatively, and non-Muslims are not allowed to enter the prayer hall.

⑧ South Cathedral
MAP J6 ▪ 141 Qian Men Xi Dajie ▪ Subway: Xuanwu Men ▪ English Mass: 10:30am Sun

Known officially in Beijing as the Cathedral of the Immaculate Conception, this was the first Catholic church to be built in the city. It stands on the site of the residence of the first Jesuit missionary to reach the city, Matteo Ricci. Arriving in 1601, the Italian won the favor of the Wanli emperor by presenting him with gifts of European curiosities such as mathematical instruments and clocks. Ricci founded the church in 1605, although the present building dates to 1904, replacing a structure that was burned down during the Boxer Rebellion. It has some fine stained-glass windows.

⑨ Natural History Museum
MAP E6 ▪ 126 Tangqiao Nan Dajie ▪ 6702 7702 ▪ Subway: Zhushikou, then walk ▪ Open 9am–5pm Tue–Sun ▪ www.bmnh.org.cn

This overbearing piece of 1950s architecture houses a great collection of dinosaur skeletons, as well as stuffed pandas and other animals. There are also fish, both dead (preserved in formaldehyde) and alive (in the aquarium).

Ancient Architecture Museum

⑩ Ancient Architecture Museum
MAP D6 ▪ 21 Dongjing Lu ▪ 6304 5608 ▪ Bus 15 to Nanwei Lu ▪ Open 9am–4pm Tue–Sun ▪ Adm (audio guide ¥10, plus ¥100 deposit)

Housed in the Hall of Jupiter, part of the Xiannong Tan temple complex, this museum focuses on the ancient construction techniques of Beijing buildings, all illuminated with detailed models. A fascinating 3D plan shows the city as it was in 1949, its city walls and gates largely intact.

A DAY SOUTH OF TIAN'AN MEN SQUARE

▶ MORNING

Start on Tian'an Men Square, at the southeast corner beside the stripey brick Old Qian Men Railway Station, built by the British in 1906, partly to bring military forces straight to the assistance of foreigners in case of a repeat of the siege of the Boxers. It's now a **Railway Museum** (see p18). Venture east along Dong Jiao Min Xiang into the **Legation Quarter** to visit the **Police Museum** (see p40). On leaving, head south to Qian Men Dong Dajie and walk back west for a glimpse of the Beijing of the future at the **Beijing Planning Exhibition Hall** (see p75). From the museum, head into the *hutongs* toward Dazhalan for some crispy roast duck at **Deyuan** (see p79).

AFTERNOON

Head east along **Dazhalan Jie** (see p75). This is a great place for specialty shops. Located down the first alley is 400-year-old **Liubiju** (see p78), selling a vast array of pickles. **Ruifuxiang** (see p78) dates from 1893 and is renowned for silks. **Tongrentang Pharmacy** (see p78) has been in business since 1669, while Zhangyiyuan Chazhuang has been trading teas since the early 20th century. For an unconventional tea-tasting experience, head west to **Alice's Tea House** (see p79), then grab a spicy Hunan dinner at **The Southern Fish** (see p79).

See map on pp74–5 ←

Shops

Souvenir shop on Liulichang

1 Liulichang
This picturesque street (see p75) was renovated in the 1980s to give it an Old China look. It's still fun to browse for antiques and art supplies.

2 Hong Qiao Market
MAP F6 ▪ 36 Hong Qiao Lu
▪ 6713 3354 ▪ Open 8:30am–7pm daily
Specializing in pearls and precious stones, this indoor market also sells clothes, bags, and shoes (see p60).

3 Panjiayuan Antique Market
MAP E5 ▪ Panjiayuan Qiao ▪ 6775 2405
▪ Subway: Panjiayuan
▪ Open 8:30am–6pm Mon–Fri, 4:30am–6pm Sat & Sun
Set the alarm for dawn for a treasure hunt down at Beijing's sprawling flea market (see p61).

Antiques from Panjiayuan

4 Beijing Curio City
MAP E5 ▪ 21 Dong San Huan Nan Lu ▪ 6774 7711 ▪ Subway: Panjiayuan ▪ Open 10am–7pm daily
Just south of Panjiayuan, Curio City has four levels of antiques, porcelain, carpets, Buddhist statues and jewelry.

5 Neiliansheng
MAP E5 ▪ 34 Dazhalan Jie
▪ 6301 4863
Beijing's best-known shoe store, in business since 1853 is known for supplying footwear to Chairman Mao.

6 Maliandao Tea Street
MAP B6 ▪ 11 Maliandao Lu, Guang'anmen Wai ▪ Bus 46, 89, 414, or special line 27
▪ Open 9am–7pm daily
This three-floor market (literally, "tea street") could also be called "Little Fujian," so ubiquitous are traders from China's tea capital. It's Beijing's best place to buy or sample an incredible variety of teas.

7 Ruifuxiang
MAP E5 ▪ 5 Dazhalan Dong Jie
▪ 6303 5764 ▪ Open 9am–9pm daily
Silk has been sold on this precise spot since 1893. Tailors can create pretty blouses and qipaos (the old-style Chinese dress).

8 Qian Xiang Yi Silk Store
MAP E5 ▪ 5 Zhubaoshi, Qianmen Jie ▪ 6301 6658
This venerable store is said to date back to 1840. Prices for quality tailoring and ready-made clothes are reasonable.

9 Tongrentang Pharmacy
MAP E5 ▪ 24 Qian Men Dazhalan
Founded in 1669, Tongrentang is China's oldest pharmacy. The store stocks thousands of traditional medicines, some of which were used in the imperial court.

10 Liubiju
MAP E5 ▪ 3 Liangshidian Jie
A jar of Chinese pickles may not be high on your list of essentials, but a visit to this colorful, nearly 500-year-old shop should be.

See map on pp74–5

Restaurants and Teahouses

PRICE CATEGORIES

For the equivalent of a meal for two made up of a range of dishes, served with two glasses of wine, and including service.

¥ under ¥250 ¥¥ ¥250–¥500
¥¥¥ over ¥500

1 Soloist Coffee Co

MAP E5 ■ 39 Yangmeizhu Xiejie, near Maishi Jie ■ 5711 1717 ■ ¥

Soloist's coffee is roasted in-house, and wait staff are friendly coffee snobs who make perfect brews.

2 Suzuki Kitchen

MAP E5 ■ 16 Yangmeizhu Xie Jie, Dongcheng District ■ 6313 5409 ■ ¥

A small and cozy restaurant that serves great Japanese hotpot and curries at very reasonable prices.

3 Liqun Roast Duck Restaurant

MAP M6 ■ 11 Beixianfeng Hutong, enter via Zhengyi Lu ■ 6705 5578 ■ ¥¥

Beijing duck at this little courtyard restaurant is usually sublime, despite the rough-and-ready ambience.

4 Lao She Teahouse

MAP L6 ■ 3 Qian Men Xi Dajie ■ 6303 6830 ■ ¥¥

A fascinating old-style Beijing teahouse that hosts acrobatics and opera shows in a small upstairs theater. It's a touristy spot, but worth a visit nonetheless.

5 Qian Men Quanjude

MAP L6 ■ 32 Qian Men Dajie ■ 6511 2418 ■ ¥¥

A famous Quanjude restaurant; Call by for take-away duck pancakes.

6 The Southern Fish

49, Gongmenkou Toutiao ■ ¥¥

In the heart of the *hutongs*, in a chic courtyard, lies this popular place serving spicy Hunan classics. Book ahead or take your chances *(see p57)*.

7 Alice's Tea House

81 Tieshuxie Jie, Xicheng District ■ 6908 0852 ■ ¥

The friendly owner, Alice, will take you through the varieties of Chinese tea and the tea ceremony. Book ahead.

8 Deyuan

MAP E5 ■ 57 Dashilan Xi Dajie, Xicheng District ■ 6308 5371 ■ ¥¥

One of the better places to enjoy duck with locals, not tourists – and at bargain prices, too.

9 Lost Heaven

MAP E4 ■ 23 Qian Men Dong Dajie ■ 8516 2698 ■ ¥¥¥

A luxuriously designed restaurant serving a tangy fusion of Yunnan, Thai, and Burmese cuisines.

10 Lao Beijing Zhajiang Mian Da Wang

MAP E5 ■ 56 Dong Xinglong Jie ■ 6701 1116 ■ ¥

A bustling eatery selling traditional Beijing snacks. Cheap and tasty fare.

Decorative exterior, Lao She Teahouse

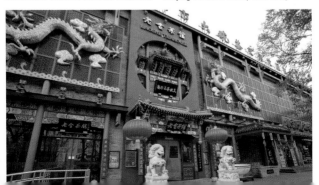

TOP 10 North of the Forbidden City

An almost contiguous run of lakes, either set in parkland or surrounded by charming *hutongs*, stretches through the neighborhood north of the Forbidden City. It's a rewarding area to explore on foot: along its narrow streets you'll find ancient temples and grand old courtyard residences, and the recent influx of restaurants, bars, and shops has not spoiled the picturesque setting.

Boating in Bei Hai Park

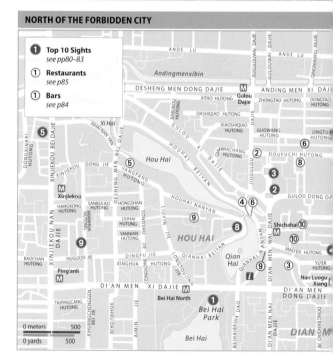

NORTH OF THE FORBIDDEN CITY

1 Bei Hai Park

A classic imperial garden, Bei Hai was a summer playground for successive dynasties that ruled from the neighboring Forbidden City. Now open to the public, it is thronged by locals who come here to socialize. There are a couple of small temples, a fine, small ornamental garden, and a noted restaurant. This is arguably the loveliest of Beijing's many fine city parks (see pp24–5).

2 Drum Tower

MAP E2 ■ Gulou Dong Dajie ■ 8403 6706 ■ Subway: Zhonglou ■ Open 8:30am–9pm daily (Nov–Mar: to 4:30pm) ■ Adm

Drum towers (gu lou) were once found in all major Chinese towns. They housed large drums that were beaten to mark the hour, keeping the city's civil servants on time for work. This structure dates to 1420. Visitors can inspect some 25 drums here and be

Inside the 15th-century Drum Tower

entertained by drummers delivering skin-thumping performances. Call ahead for performance times.

3 Bell Tower

MAP E1 ■ Gulou Dong Dajie ■ 8403 6706 ■ Subway: Zhonglou ■ Open 8:30am–9pm daily (Nov–Mar: to 4:30pm) ■ Adm

Dating from 1745, this replaces an earlier tower that burned down. The heavy bell it contains used to be rung to mark the closing of the city gates in the evening. During Spring Festival visitors are allowed to ring the bell for a donation of ¥100. The views from both the Drum and Bell Towers are well worth the exhausting climb.

4 Nan Luogu Xiang

MAP E2

Close to the Drum Tower, Nan Luogu Xiang is arguably Beijing's hippest hutong. Though in line for redevelopment work, it still has a traditional feel, and is home to small hotels, interesting clothing and craft boutiques, and a number of cafés and bars. Baochao Hutong, nearby, is a hipster hangout that's popular with the locals.

Boutique in Nan Luogu Xiang

CONFUCIUS

Born during an age of war, Confucius (551–479 BC) was prompted by the suffering around him to develop a philosophy built on the principle of virtue. Finding no audience among his native rulers, he set off in search of a ruler who would apply his rules of governance. He never found such a person and died unrecognized.

5 Xu Beihong Memorial Museum

MAP D1 ▪ 53 Xinjiekou Bei Dajie ▪ 6225 2187 ▪ Subway: Jishuitan ▪ Open 9am–4pm Tue–Sun ▪ Adm (audio guide ¥10, plus ¥100 deposit)

Set back from the road with a sign on top in green characters, this museum is dedicated to the man regarded as the founder of modern Chinese painting. It exhibits a collection of the lively watercolors of horses that made Xu Beihong (1885–1953) internationally famous.

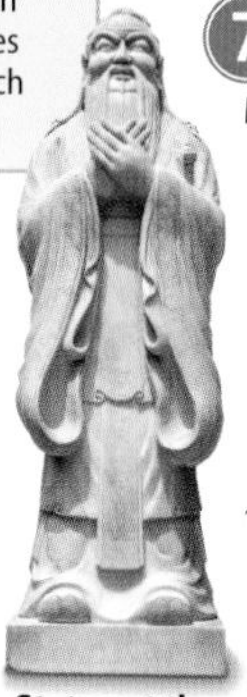

Statue at the Confucius Temple

6 Lama Temple (Yonghe Gong)

About a 30-minute walk east of the Drum and Bell Towers, or just a few minutes south of the Yonghe Gong subway station, the Lama Temple (see pp20–21) is Beijing's largest working temple complex. It is filled every day with about an equal number of visitors and worshipers.

7 Confucius Temple (Kong Miao)

MAP F1 ▪ 13 Guozi Jian Jie ▪ 8402 7224 ▪ Subway: Yonghe Gong ▪ Open 8:30am–5pm daily ▪ Adm

Located to the west of the Lama Temple, the Confucius Temple was built in 1302 during the Mongol Yuan dynasty, and expanded in 1906. Around 200 ancient stelae stand in the courtyard in front of the main hall, inscribed with the names of those who successfully passed the imperial civil service exams. On a marble terrace inside the hall are statues of Confucius and a number of his disciples.

8 Hou Hai

The most visitor-friendly neighborhood of Beijing, Hou Hai (see pp26–7) consists of three joined lakes surrounded by an expansive and labyrinthine sprawl of age-old

Red-and-gold pavilion at the Lama Temple (Yonghegong)

Willow-lined lake in Hou Hai

hutongs (alleys). Visit to admire a handful of well-preserved mansions, as well as for the opportunity to see a more humble form of Beijing life as it has been lived for centuries.

⑨ Former Residence of Mei Lanfang

MAP D2 ▪ 9 Huguosi Jie ▪ 8322 3598 ▪ Subway: Jishuitan ▪ Open 9am–4pm Tue–Sun ▪ Adm ▪ www.meilanfang.com.cn

This was the home of Beijing Opera's greatest ever performer (1894–1961). The rear rooms have been left with their traditional furniture as it was when he died. Others contain a hagiographic account of his life, as well as diagrams of the stylized movements required by the form, and a video of Mei, aged 61 but still playing the young girl roles for which he was famous *(see p52)*.

⑩ Di Tan Park

MAP F1 ▪ North of Lama Temple ▪ Subway: Yonghe Gong ▪ Open 6am–8:30pm daily (Nov–Mar: to 9pm daily) ▪ Adm ▪ www.dtpark.com

The park was named for the Altar of Earth (Di Tan), which was a venue for imperial sacrifices. The altar's square shape represents the earth. These days, the park is always full of pensioners strolling, chatting, and exercising. A lively temple fair is held here at Chinese New Year.

A DAY IN THE HUTONGS

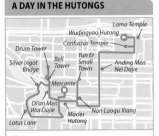

▶ MORNING

Take an early morning stroll along Wudingyao Hutong, where you can have breakfast at one of the cafés. Then continue on to the **Lama Temple** *(see pp20–21)*. On leaving, cross over the main road and pass under the *pailou* (gate) at the entrance to Guozi Jian Jie for the **Confucius Temple**. Afterward, sample Guozi Jian's many cafés, or browse through the city's best traditional craft shops. At the western end of Guozi Jian Jie turn left onto **Anding Men Nei Dajie**, a wide, shop-filled avenue, follow it south across Jiaodaokuo Dong Dajie and take a right on Dongmianhua Hutong, one of the more vibrant of the city's old alleys. Take the first left onto **Nan Luogu Xiang** *(see p81)*, cross Gu Lou Dong Dajie to Bei Luogu Xiang, and stop for a Yunnan lunch on the terrace of **Yun Er Small Town** *(see p85)* before hitting the boutiques.

AFTERNOON

Head west along **Mao'er Hutong** until you reach **Di'an Men Wai Dajie**, where you turn right and up the street for the **Drum Tower** and the **Bell Tower** *(see p81)*. Climb the towers to see the route you've just taken. Retrace your steps back down Di'an Men Wai Dajie taking the very first right, a tiny opening (usually marked by waiting taxis) leading into Yandai Xie Jie *(see p27)*. At the end of this crooked alley is the **Silver Ingot Bridge** *(see p26)*; cross and bear left for **Lotus Lane** *(see p27)*. For dinner, head east back into the *hutongs* for a cozy Italian meal at **Mercante** *(see p57)*.

See map on pp80–81

Bars

Capital Spirits Baijiu Bar & Distillery

(5) The Tiki Bungalow
MAP F2 ▪ 46 Fangjia Hutong

This roomy, popular *hutong* bar brings the tropics to Beijing. There are over 60 cocktails, and the staff have an intimate knowledge of rum.

(6) Modernista
MAP E1 ▪ 44 Baochao Hutong ▪ 136 9142 5744

Keep the winter chill at bay with the delicious warm wine served at this 1920s-themed jazz and piano bar *(see p59)*. In summer, try their sangria.

(7) Arch
MAP F2 ▪ 3 Zhangzizhong Lu ▪ 6409 3319

An intimate, classy bar tucked in a corner away from the bustle of central Beijing. Enjoy their potent cocktails made from the choicest of liquors.

(8) Mai
MAP E1 ▪ 40 Bei Luogu Xiang ▪ 138 1125 2641

Visit this tiny bar *(see p58)* to choose from a wide range of cocktails prepared by a trained mixologist.

(9) East Shore Live Jazz Café
MAP E2 ▪ 2 Qianhai Nanyan Lu ▪ 8403 2131

Opened by famous jazzman Liu Yuan, this bar has steep wooden stairs, four walls of floor-to-ceiling windows and a roof terrace, plus live music.

(1) Capital Spirits Baijiu Bar & Distillery
MAP F2 ▪ 16 Xinsi Hutong ▪ 6409 3319

With a stripped-down bar and a cozy lounge, this remodeled traditional *siheyuan* offers great views. Try the house gin, vodka or fiery Chinese baijiu, fresh from the copper still.

(2) Nuo Yan Rice Wine
MAP F2 ▪ 7 Banqiao South Alley ▪ 134 2628 6012

With a sophisticated air about it and a unique, expansive rice wine list, Nuo Yan has secured a place among the top bars in town. You can also learn about rice wine production here.

(3) Ramo
MAP F1 ▪ 64 Fangjia Hutong ▪ 8403 5004

A casual bar with minimalist, polished-concrete decor, this place is often filled with young foreign residents. It serves decent pizza, and a variety of imported ales.

(4) Mao Mao Chong
MAP E2 ▪ 12 Banchang Hutong, off Jiaodaokou Nanje ▪ 6405 5718

This laid-back and affordable *hutong* bar offers a selection of creative cocktails, plus gourmet pizzas. The owner is friendly and speaks English.

(10) Great Leap Brewery #6
MAP E2 ▪ 6 Doujiao Hutong, off Di'an Men Wai Dajie ▪ 5717 1399

Located on a quiet *hutong*, this craft beer pioneer offers a pleasant courtyard and comfy sofas.

Restaurants

PRICE CATEGORIES

For the equivalent of a meal for two made up of a range of dishes, served with two glasses of wine, and including service.

¥ under ¥250   ¥¥ ¥250–¥500
¥¥¥ over ¥500

1 **Dali Courtyard**
MAP E2 ▪ 67 Xiaojingchang Hutong, Gulou Dong Dajie ▪ 8404 1430 ▪ ¥¥

This charming, little, laid-back restaurant (see p57) is one of the city's most unique outdoor venue and perfect for meals in summer in a beautiful courtyard. Book ahead for the spicy Yunnan dishes.

2 **Cafe Sambal**
MAP E1 ▪ 43 Doufuchi Hutong, off Jiugulou Dajie ▪ 6400 4875 ▪ ¥¥

An old-style courtyard house serves exquisite dishes cooked by a talented and creative Malaysian chef. The focus here is on modern Malaysian cuisine, with an influence from Southeast Asia.

3 **Georg**
45 Dongbuyaqiao Hutong, nr Dianmen Dajie ▪ 8408 5300 ▪ ¥¥¥

Run by the Danish brand Georg Jensen, this place (see p56) attracts Beijing's A-list crowd. European dishes created with Scandanavian sophistication are on offer here.

4 **Kaorou Ji**
MAP E2 ▪ 14 Qianhai Dong Yan ▪ 6404 2554 ▪ ¥¥

This exquisite restaurant majors in Qingzhen– Hui or Muslim – cuisine, which means mutton. The specialty here is barbe-cued lamb, and sesame seed bread.

5 **Kong Yiji**
MAP E2 ▪ Desheng Men Nei Dajie ▪ 6618 4917 ▪ ¥

A lovely lakeside restaurant with a range of exquisite dishes from the Yangzi River delta.

6 **Nuage**
MAP E2 ▪ 22 Qian Hai Dong Yan ▪ 6401 9581 ▪ ¥

A well-respected Vietnamese restaurant with a lovely location just south of the Silver Ingot Bridge.

7 **Yun Er Small Town**
MAP E1 ▪ 84 Bei Luogu Xiang ▪ ¥

A cheaper option, Yun Er (see p57) has a rooftop terrace and the best Yunnan fried cheese in town.

8 **Toast at the Orchid**
MAP E2 ▪ 65 Baochao Hutong, Dongcheng District ▪ 8404 4818 ▪ ¥¥¥

Toast (see p56) boasts a relaxed, ambience and fusion food that blends flavours of the Middle-East with those of Asia and North Africa.

9 **Mei Fu Jia Yan**
MAP D2 ▪ 24 Daxiangfeng Hutong ▪ 6612 6845 ▪ ¥¥¥

This restaurant is set within a gorgeous courtyard house lavishly filled with antiques. Set menus of sweet and rich Shanghainese cuisine are also available.

10 **Mercante**
4 Fangzhuanchang Hutong, Dongcheng District ▪ 8402 5098 ▪ ¥¥¥

This little Italian restaurant serves a top selection of dishes, and also has an expansive wine list to choose from (see p57).

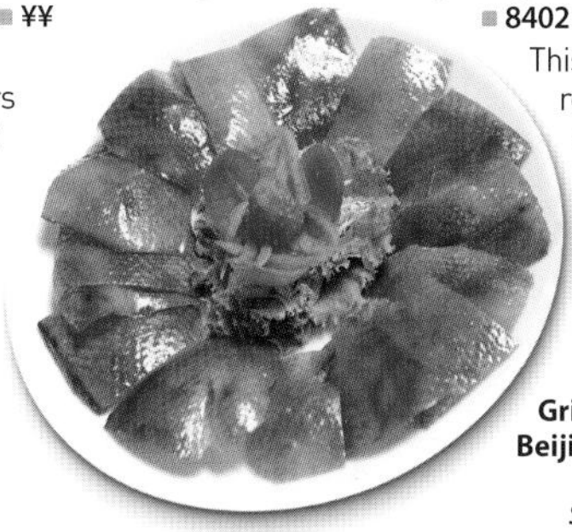

Grill skin Beijing duck

See map on pp80–81

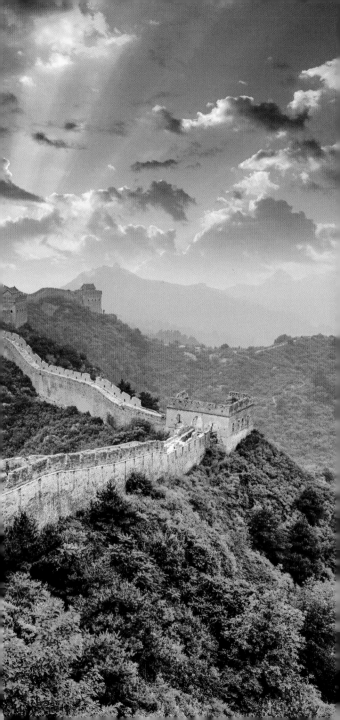

TOP10 Eastern Beijing

East of central Beijing, in a corridor between the Second and Third Ring Roads, is the district of Chaoyang. It's not an area that is particularly old and it doesn't have very many significant monuments, but it is home to two main clusters of international embassies, and it is where a large proportion of the city's expatriate community chooses to live. As a result, Chaoyang is the city's entertainment and nightlife center, and, for the visitor, it is the prime area for eating and shopping.

CCTV Tower, Central Business District

EASTERN BEIJING

1 Top 10 Sights
see pp88–91

1 Restaurants
see p93

1 Shops, Markets, and Malls
see p92

Previous pages The Great Wall of China at Jinshanling

Courtyard of the Ancient Observatory

1 Ancient Observatory
MAP G4 ■ 6524 2202
■ Subway: Jianguo Men ■ Open
9am–5pm Tue–Sun ■ Adm

Dating to 1442, Beijing's observatory is one of the oldest in the world. In fact, there was an even earlier Yuan-dynasty (1279–1368) observatory also located on this site but no trace of that remains. Today, a collection of reproduction astronomical devices lies in the courtyard, some of them decorated with fantastic Chinese designs. There are more impressive instruments on the roof.

2 Central Business District (CBD)
MAP H4 ■ Subway: Jianguo Men, Yong'an Li, Guomao or Dawanglu

The Central Business District is Beijing's business hub, housing more than 60 percent of the city's foreign-funded companies. Marked by the CCTV Tower in the northeast and by the Twin Towers of the China World Trade Center in the southwest, the area is also home

to about half of the city's luxury hotels and two of its glitziest shopping malls, China World and Parkview Green (see p92).

3 Blue Zoo Beijing
MAP G3 ■ South gate of Workers' Stadium ■ 6591 3397
■ Subway: Chaoyang Men ■ Open 8am–8pm daily (Dec–Apr: 8:30am–6:30pm daily) ■ Adm; children under 3 ft (1 m) free ■ www. bluezoo.com.cn

Not a zoo at all, but a modern aquarium, reckoned to be the best of its kind in Asia. The main attraction is a central tank holding thousands of fish, plus there are also 18 additional tanks with specifically themed displays (see p49).

4 Sanlitun
MAP H2 ■ Subway: Tuanjiehu

Beijing's main expat-friendly shopping, dining, and drinking district is centered around Taikoo Li and Nali Patio on Sanlitun Bei Lu, and around the Workers' Stadium on Gongren Tiyuchang Bei Lu. It has a high concentration of international restaurants (see p93) and lots of boutique shopping (see p92). Streets around here, although modern, are tree-lined and, with plenty of cafés for refreshment stops, it is a very pleasant district to wander in.

Shop-lined street in Sanlitun

5 Southeast Corner Watchtower (Dong Bian Men)

MAP G5 ■ South of Jianguo Men Nei Dajie ■ 8512 1554 ■ Subway: Jianguo Men ■ Open 8am–4:30pm daily ■ Adm

Just south of the Second Ring Road, a chunk of the old city wall survives, including the 15th-century Dong Bian Men watchtower. Visitors can climb onto the battlements, walk along the wall and see the graffiti carved by soldiers during the Boxer Rebellion.

Southeast Corner Watchtower

6 Laitai Flower Market

9 Maizidian Xi Lu, Chaoyang District ■ 6463 5588 ■ Open 9am–5:30pm daily (to 6pm Fri–Sun)

This massive glass-fronted building flanked by stone elephants is much more than a flower market. Wander the jungle-like rows, or browse shops for quirky furniture, ceramics, cut bamboo, decorative boxes, and even tropical fish. Wear layers – it can get steamy in here.

7 Ghost Street

MAP F2 ■ Subway: Beixingqiao

Gui Jie, or Ghost Street, is a 1-mile (2-km) stretch of Dong Zhi Men Nei Dajie that come nightfall is jammed with cars double-parked outside its 100 or so restaurants, many of which open 24 hours. The air smells like Sichuan peppercorn and chilies while most establishments favor corny, old-China decor with plenty

ALTARED CITY

Ri Tan Park's Altar of the Sun is one of eight such cosmologically aligned structures, along with the Altar of Heaven (Tian Tan; see pp16–17), the Altar of Agriculture (Xiannong Tan; now part of the Ancient Architecture Museum; see p77), the Altar of the Moon in the west of the city, the Altar of Earth (Di Tan, see p83), the Altar of the Country in Zhong Shan Park, the Altar of the Silkworm in Bei Hai Park, and the lost Altar of the Gods of Heaven.

of red lacquer and pagoda motifs, and waitresses in silk tunics. This is the home of one of the most popular dishes in Beijing: the hot pot, although all regional Chinese cuisines are represented here.

8 Workers' Stadium

MAP G2 ■ Gongren Tiyuchang Bei Lu ■ 6522 5665 ■ Subway: Dong Si Shi Tiao

With an estimated capacity of 72,000, the stadium is home to Beijing's premier soccer club, Beijing Guo'an, and it is the city's main venue for large-scale rock and pop concerts. Perplexingly, it is also a hub of Beijing nightlife, with numerous clubs and bars clustered around its north and west gates, and some very good restaurants too. Even oldies get in on the act, with mass open-air dancing taking place on the forecourt of the north gate most summer evenings.

9 Dong Yue Miao
MAP G3 ■ 141 Chaoyang
Men Wai Dajie ■ 6551 0151
■ Subway: Dongdaqiao ■ Open
8:30am–4:30pm Tue–Sun ■ Adm

This colorful, active temple dating
to the early 14th century is tended
by Daoist monks. The main courtyard
leads into the Hall of Tai Shan, with
statues of gods and their attendants.

Statues in the Dong Yue Miao temple

10 Ri Tan Park
MAP G4 ■ Guanghua Lu ■ 8561
6301 ■ Subway: Jianguo Men ■ Open
6am–10pm daily (Nov–Mar: to 9pm)

One of the city's oldest parks, Ri Tan
was laid out around a sacrificial altar
in the 16th century. The round altar
remains, ringed by a wall, but this is
very much a living park, filled daily
with people walking and exercising.
The park is well maintained and is
surrounded by restaurants and cafés.

Red lanterns hanging in Ri Tan Park

A WALK FROM RI TAN PARK TO SANLITUN

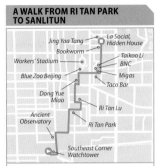

▶ MORNING

Start the day at the **Southeast
Corner Watchtower**, for an aerial
view from one of Beijing's last
remaining city walls. Walk to the
Ancient Observatory (see p89) to
see ancient brass instruments
(and another rooftop view). Keep
heading north, but take a break in
Ri Tan Park, one of the city's more
picturesque green spots. The park
is home to a lake and the ruins of
a sacrificial altar, but it is better
known for the countless locals
who come to exercise, fly kites,
do morning tai chi, or to simply
enjoy the view.

AFTERNOON

Head out of the park via the
eastern exit and grab lunch at one
of **Ri Tan Lu's** many cafés before
continuing north to the vibrant
Dong Yue Miao temple. Go to the
south gate of the **Workers'
Stadium** to visit the popular **Blue
Zoo Beijing** (see p89), then keep
heading north into **Sanlitun** (see
p89) for an afternoon of shopping
at Taikoo Li. Check out the best
Chinese designers at **BNC** (see
p92), pick up some chic ceramics
at **Spin** (see p92), and restock your
coffee-table books at **Bookworm**
(see p113). For cheap eats, try the
Taco Bar (see p93), or go to **Jing
Yaa Tang** (see p93) for something
more upmarket. Enjoy a nightcap
at **La Social** (see p58) or **Hidden
House** (see p58) before going
dancing on **Migas'** terrace (see p58).

See map on p88 ←

Shops, Markets, and Malls

① Tailor Shops in Sanlitun
MAP H2 ■ Yashow's side streets (off Gongtibeilu) and Sanlitun Xijie

The streets to the west of Taikoo Li are full of custom tailors who can accommodate your schedule.

Silk Street Market artist and vendor

② Silk Street Market
MAP G4 ■ 8 Xiushui Dongjie, Jianwai Dajie ■ 5169 9003

This five-story market is the place to get silk goods, such as ties, table-cloths, traditional clothes and dressing gowns. It is also filled with counterfeit designer goods (see p61).

③ China World Shopping Mall
MAP H4 ■ 1 Jianguo Men Wai Dajie ■ 6505 2288

The Silk Market sells the counterfeits, but this elegant shopping mall is where you come for the originals.

④ Shin Kong Place (SKP)
87 Jianguo Lu ■ 8078 8888

Opened in April 2007, Shin Kong is a temple for luxury shopping and gourmet dining. It also marked the debut appearance of many elite brands in mainland China.

⑤ Sanlitun SOHO
MAP H2 ■ South side of Gongren Tiyuchang Bei Lu ■ 5878 8888

Characterized by some colorful funnel-shaped buildings, Sanlitun SOHO is a vast complex of shopping malls, offices, hotels, and private apartments. Numerous brand stores, banks, restaurants, and cafés occupy the first floor.

⑥ Brand New China (BNC)
MAP H2 ■ NLG-09a, B1, Sanlitun Village North, 11 Sanlitun Lu ■ 6416 9045

Created by media celebrity Hung Huang, BNC celebrates Chinese fashion. Collect emerging designers' works while they're still affordable.

⑦ Parkview Green
MAP H4 ■ 9 Dongdaqiao Lu ■ 5690 7000

Chic, eco-friendly mall with a range of fashion wear and accessories – from fashionable traditional Chinese women's wear by Amelie Wang to watches and jewelry by Van Cleef & Arpels, plus displays of contemporary art and Salvador Dalí sculptures.

⑧ Spin
6 Dingfu Zhuang Xili, Chaoyang District ■ 6437 8649

These stylish ceramics are more affordable here than in Spin's other bases in Shanghai and New York. Check out the "Seven Fortune" pots.

⑨ Taikoo Li Sanlitun
MAP H2 ■ 6 Gongren Tiyuchang Bei Lu (corner Sanlitun Bei Lu) ■ 6417 6110

The upscale Village has many brand stores including Apple and Adidas, plus a range of restaurants and bars.

⑩ Jenny Lou's
MAP G3 ■ 6 Sanlitun Bei Xiang ■ 6461 6928

Expat heaven, with Dutch cheese, German bread, and French wines.

Restaurants

PRICE CATEGORIES

For the equivalent of a meal for two made up of a range of dishes, served with two glasses of wine, and including service.

¥ under ¥250   ¥¥ ¥250–¥500
¥¥¥ over ¥500

1 Jing Yaa Tang
MAP H2 ■ 1/F The Opposite House Hotel, 11 Sanlitun Bei Lu ■ 6410 5230 ■ ¥¥¥

This elegant restaurant specializes in Beijing roast duck and regional Chinese dishes such as Kung Pao chicken and dim sum.

2 Taco Bar
MAP H2 ■ Unit 10, Electrical Research Institute, Gongti Bei Lu ■ 6501 6026 ■ Closed Mon & lunch Tue–Fri ■ ¥

The fish tacos here are addictive. Add a pitcher of margarita, and you'll never want to leave.

Comfort food at Taco Bar

3 Mosto
MAP H2 ■ Nali Patio, 81 Sanlitun Bei Lu ■ 5208 6030 ■ ¥¥

A stylish restaurant (see p56) featuring Mediterranean cuisine. Try their delicious risotto and the superb cocktails served after dark.

4 Hatsune
MAP H4 ■ 2nd floor, Heqiao Building C, 8a Guanghua Dong Lu ■ 6415 3939 ■ ¥¥

A class act: this stylish Japanese restaurant has fresh fish flown in daily. The sushi is excellent.

5 Country Kitchen
MAP H3 ■ Rosewood Beijing, Jingguang Centre, 1 Chaoyangmen Dajie ■ 6597 8888 ■ ¥¥¥

The chefs here masterfully reinvent traditional Chinese recipes in an open kitchen. Be sure to try the excellent hand-pulled noodle dishes (see p57).

6 Bottega
MAP H2 ■ 18 Sanlitun Lu ■ 6416 1752 ■ ¥¥

This popular pizzeria offers pizzas and calzones with charcoal crusts made with imported ingredients.

7 Migas
MAP H2 ■ 6th Floor, Nali Patio, 81 Sanlitun Lu ■ 5208 6061 ■ ¥¥¥

Known for its rooftop bar and dance patio, Migas serves Spanish sharing plates such as salted cod and steamed eggplant, and oxtail in red wine.

8 Transit
MAP H2 ■ N4-36, 3/F The Village, North Sanlitun Bei Lu ■ 6417 9090 ■ ¥¥

Enjoy beautifully spiced Sichuan cuisine at this sophisticated but unpretentious restaurant.

9 Cai Yi Xuan
MAP H1 ■ Four Seasons Beijing, 48 Liang Ma Qiao Lu ■ 5695 8520 ■ ¥¥¥

Enjoy Beijing's best dim sums, along with top Cantonese fare (see p57).

10 Beijing Dadong Roast Duck Restaurant
MAP H2 ■ Bdg 3, Tuanjiehu Beikou, Dongsanhuan Bei Lu ■ 6582 4003 ■ ¥¥

It is the opinion of a great many Beijingers that there is no finer duck than that served here.

Beijing Dadong Roast Duck Restaurant

See map on p88

ⓣⓞⓟ Western Beijing

Xicheng, meaning "West City," is the central district west of the Forbidden City and the lakes. Beijingers think of this area as a seat of money and learning – both the Financial District and Haidian University are here. Western Beijing is best experienced as a series of half-day expeditions: a visit to the Military Museum with a look at the Millennium Monument afterward, or a trip to the aquarium followed by the Temple of the Five Pagodas. Expect to make liberal use of taxis and the subway.

Gilded bronze statue at the Capital Museum

① Capital Museum

MAP B4 ■ 16 Fuxing Men Wai Dajie, Xicheng ■ 6337 0491 ■ Subway: Muxidi ■ Open 9am–5pm Tue–Sun ■ en.capitalmuseum.org.cn

The popular Capital Museum celebrates China's civilization in general and Beijing's history in particular. The five-story building is easily recognizable thanks to its huge bronze cylinder. Exhibits include porcelain art, calligraphy, Buddha statues, furniture, and crafts. Reserve online.

WESTERN BEIJING

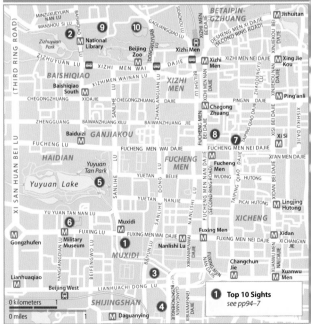

> ① Top 10 Sights
> see pp94–7

Immense reading room in the National Library of China

2 National Library of China

MAP A1 ▪ 33 Zhongguancun Nandajie ▪ 8854 5426 ▪ Subway: National Library ▪ Open 9am–9pm Mon–Fri, 9am–5pm Sat & Sun (except pub hols) ▪ www.nlc.gov.cn

One of the five biggest libraries in the world, the National Library of China has been expanded to accommodate its collection of approximately 12 million books. The building's floating roof houses the Digital Library. Most books are reference only, but visitors can request a reader's pass.

3 White Cloud Temple

MAP B4 ▪ 6 Baiyun Guan Jie, off Lianhuachi Dong Lu ▪ 6346 3531 ▪ Subway: Nanlishi Lu ▪ Open 8:30am–4:30pm daily (Oct 8–Apr: to 4pm) ▪ Adm

The first temple on this site was founded in AD 739 and burnt down in 1166. Since that time, it has been repeatedly destroyed and rebuilt. It even survived being used as a factory during the Cultural Revolution. The shrines, pavilions, and courtyards that make up the compound today date mainly from the Ming and Qing dynasties. Monks here are followers of Daoism and sport distinctive top-knots. Each Chinese New Year this is the venue for one of the city's most popular temple fairs, with performers, artisans, and traders.

4 Temple of Heavenly Tranquility (Tianning Si)

MAP B5 ▪ Guann'gan Men Nanbinhe Lu ▪ Subway: Daguanying, then taxi

This temple, built in the 5th century AD, is one of the city's oldest. The striking octagonal pagoda was added in the early 12th century. The bottom of the pagoda is decorated with carved arch patterns, symbolizing Sumeru, the mountain of the gods. Above are 13 levels of eaves, with no doors or windows – the pagoda is without stairs inside or outside and is, in fact, solid.

Temple of Heavenly Tranquility

Brightly colored flower beds in full bloom at Yuyuan Tan Park

5 Yuyuan Tan Park
MAP A3 ■ Xisanhuan Lu ■ Subway: Military Museum ■ Open Dec–Mar 6:30am–7pm daily; Apr, May & Sep–Nov 6am–8:30pm; Jun–Aug 6am– 9:30pm ■ Adm

Lovely Jade Lake Park is at its most beautiful during cherry-blossom season. Rent a boat and traverse the massive lakes, go for a swim, or grab a snack from the food stalls and have a picnic – unusually for Beijing – on the grass.

6 Military Museum of the Chinese People's Revolution
MAP A4 ■ 9 Fuxing Lu ■ 6686 6244 ■ Subway: Military Museum ■ Open 8am–5pm daily

Vast halls of hardware from the Cold War-era, including lots of silvery fighter planes and tanks, fill the first floor of this interesting military museum. The floor upstairs has exhibitions on historic conflicts, including the Opium Wars and Boxer Rebellion. Unfortunately, there is very little labeling in English. What isn't mentioned is that the museum is close to the Muxidi intersection, scene of a massacre of civilians by the Chinese army during the demo-cracy protests of 1989. To gain entry into the museum, ID is required.

Statue in Miaoying Temple White Dagoba

7 Miaoying Temple White Dagoba (Baita Si)
MAP C3 ■ 171 Fucheng Men Nei Dajie ■ 6616 6099 ■ Subway: Fucheng Men ■ Open 9am–4:30pm daily ■ Adm

Celebrated for its tall, Tibetan-style white *dagoba* (stupa), this temple dates to 1271, when Beijing was under Mongol rule. The temple is also noted for its fascinating collection of thousands of Tibetan Buddhist statues.

8 Lu Xun Museum
MAP C3 ■ 19 Gong Men Kou Er Tiao, off Fucheng Men Nei Dajie ■ 6616 4080 ■ Subway: Fucheng Men ■ Open 9am–4pm Tue–Sun

Lu Xun is regarded as the father of modern Chinese literature, responsible for such

BUDDHISM IN CHINA

Buddhism started in India and probably came to China along the Silk Road. The earliest sign of the religion is linked to the founding of the White Horse Temple near the old capital of Luoyang in AD 68. Buddhism surged in popularity during periods of instability, when Confucianism's veneration for authority did not sit well with the populace. It was eventually adopted by China's rulers.

ground-breaking works as "Diary of a Madman" and "The True Story of Ah Q". This is the house in which he lived from 1924 to 1926. The rooms display artifacts relating to his life and there's also an adjacent exhibition hall with more than 10,000 letters, journals, photographs, and other personal objects.

9 Temple of the Five Pagodas

MAP B1 ■ 24 Wuta Si Cun ■ 6217 3836 ■ Subway: National Museum or Xizhi Men ■ Open 8:30am–5pm Tue–Sun ■ Adm

This temple displays obvious Indian influences. Built in the early 15th century, it honors the Indian monk who came to China and presented the emperor with five golden Buddhas. The pagodas sport elaborate carvings of curvaceous females, as well as the customary Buddhas. Also here is the Beijing Art Museum of Stone Carvings, with 2,000 decorative stelae.

Close encounters in Beijing Aquarium

10 Beijing Aquarium

MAP B2 ■ 108 Gao Liang Qiao Xijie ■ 6217 6655 ■ Open 9am–5:30pm daily (Nov–Mar: 10am–4:30pm daily) ■ Adm ■ www.bj-sea.com

Located in a corner of the zoo is this conch shell-shaped building. It is reputedly the largest inland aquarium in the world, with massive tanks containing thousands of weird, wonderful fish, plus a shark tank, coral reefs and an "Amazon rainforest." Both children and adults love this place.

WAR AND PEACE

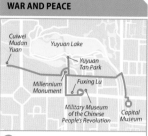

▶ MORNING

Even if you're no big fan of mechanized heavy armor, the **Military Museum of the Chinese People's Revolution** is worth a visit. Exhibits begin with the technology that made China one of the world's first military superpowers, including the "Flying Dragon," an early form of missile launcher. One room is devoted to the gifts that have been bestowed on China's army chiefs and leaders, such as a pistol presented to Chairman Mao by Fidel Castro. Mao's limousine is displayed on the first floor, and one hall is devoted to statues and assorted representations of the Communist Party's great and good. It all makes for a fascinating insight into the mentality of late 20th-century China.

AFTERNOON

Leaving the museum, walk west along Fuxing Lu and take the first right. You will see the **Millennium Monument** and, behind it, **Yuyuan Tan Park**, a relaxing place for a stroll. Pick up a snack from one of the vendors here and have a picnic, or head out to **Cuiwei Mudan Yuan** (3rd Floor, Cui Wei Da Sha, 2 Hua Yuan Lu) for hot pot before continuing on Fuxing Men Wai Dajie toward Muxidi and the **Capital Museum** (see p94). Audio self-guided tours in Chinese and English are available at the entrance. Don't miss the Peking Opera exhibition on the top floor, or the short film on Beijing's urban development, screened in the auditorium on the first floor.

See map on p94 ←

🔟 Greater Beijing

Beijing is vast. Although you could spend all your time without ever straying too far from the area around Tian'an Men Square, you would be missing out on a lot. Sights in the northwest of the city include the unmissable Summer Palace, the intoxicating hillside Xiang Shan Park and the haunting ruins of the Yuanming Yuan, or Old Summer Palace. It's worth trying to squeeze all three into one day's sightseeing. For fans of contemporary urban culture, the 798 Art District in Beijing's northeast is a must, and you can drop in on the markets and bars around Sanlitun on the way back into town.

The lakeside Summer Palace

① Summer Palace

It's only a short bus or taxi ride from Bagou subway station to the unmissable Summer Palace *(see pp28–9)*. The grounds are arranged as a microcosm of nature, with hills and water complemented by bridges temples, and walkways. It manages to be both fanciful and harmonious at the same time.

GREATER BEIJING

Ruins at Yuanming Yuan (Old Summer Palace)

② Yuanming Yuan (Old Summer Palace)

28 Qinghua Xi Lu ■ 6262 8501
■ Subway: Yuanming Yuan Park
■ Open 7am–7pm daily (Sep & Oct: to 6:30pm; Nov–Mar: to 5:30pm) ■ Adm
■ www.yuanmingyuanpark.cn

The palace's name can be translated as "Garden of Perfect Brightness." It was the largest and most elaborate of all the summer palaces of the Qing era. It once contained private imperial residences, pleasure pavilions, a vast imperial ancestral shrine, Buddhist temples, and canals and lakes. The Qianlong emperor even added a group of European-style palaces designed by Jesuit missionary-artists serving in the Qing court. Today, only graceful ruins remain, after the ravaging effects of the Second Opium War (1856–60). A museum displays images and models of the place as it was.

③ Xiang Shan Park

Wofosi Lu ■ 6259 1264
■ Bus: 331 from Summer Palace or 634 from Xizhi Men ■ Open 6am–6:30pm daily (Jul & Aug: to 7pm; mid-Nov–Mar: to 6pm)
■ Adm ■ www.xiangshan park.com

The wooded parkland area, also known as Fragrant Hills Park, is 2 miles (3 km) west of the Summer Palace. It offers fine views from Incense Burner Peak, which is accessible by a chairlift (for a fee). Close to the park's main gate is the Azure Clouds Temple (Biyun Si), guarded by the menacing deities Heng and Ha in the Mountain Gate Hall. A series of halls leads to the Sun Yat Sen Memorial Hall, where the revolutionary leader's coffin was stored in 1925, before being taken to his final resting place in Nanjing.

④ Great Bell Temple (Dazhong Temple)

MAP B1 ■ 31A Beisanhuan Xi Lu
■ 6255 0819 ■ Subway: Dazhongsi
■ Open 9am–4:30pm daily ■ Adm

This 18th-century temple follows a typical Buddhist plan, with a Heavenly Kings Hall, Main Hall, and a Guanyin Bodhisattva Hall. What distinguishes it, though, is the massive bell – (one of the world's largest – housed in the rear tower. The bell was cast between 1403 and 1424, and has Buddhist *sutras* in Chinese and Sanskrit on its surface.

Ornate bell at the Great Bell Temple

Graffiti art on a wall in the 798 Art District

⑤ 798 Art District

Although it's called the 798 Art District (see pp30–31), known locally as Da Shan Zi, Factory number 798 is only one of the several former industrial units taken over by artists and galleries. The 798 features many of Beijing's best galleries, including UCCA and Pace.

Lily pond, Beijing Botanical Gardens

⑥ Beijing Botanical Gardens

6259 1283 ■ Bus: 331 from Summer Palace or 634 from Xizhi Men ■ Open 7am–5pm daily ■ Adm ■ www.beijingbg.com

About a mile (2 km) northeast of Xiang Shan Park lie these pretty gardens, containing some 3,000 plant species and pleasant walks.

The garden's Sleeping Buddha Temple (Wofo Si) is renowned for its magnificent 15-ft (5-m) bronze statue of a reclining Buddha. China's last emperor, Pu Yi (see p13), ended his days here as a gardener.

⑦ China National Film Museum

9 Nanying Road, Caochangdi Village, Chaoyang ■ 8435 5959 ■ Bus: 418 from Dong Zhi Men ■ Open 9am–4:30pm Tue–Sun (last adm 3:30pm) ■ www.cnfm.org.cn

Reportedly the world's largest, this film museum is housed in a glass-and-steel structure and features 20 exhibition halls, an IMAX theater, a digital projection theater, and several 35mm theaters. Over 100 years of Chinese cinema are represented by 1,500 films and 4,300 stills from the works of 450 film-makers.

CHINA'S PEOPLES

China's 1.41 billion population includes about 55 different ethnic minorities, each with their own languages and, in many cases, distinctive customs. Though rich in culture, and varied, together these ethnic minorities make up only eight percent of the population, with the main group, known as Han Chinese, accounting for the rest.

8 National Aquatics Center (Water Cube)

This Olympic venue proves there is life after the Games – today, the Water Cube *(see p44)* is a popular water park, and it is earmarked to host the 2022 Winter Games' curling events. In this collaboration between Chinese and Australian architects, China drew from the classical mythology tradition of a square earth and round heaven, symbolized here by the angled building and the circular stadium. The Australians designed the bubbles, representing soap lather's natural pattern.

Science and Technology Museum

9 Science and Technology Museum

MAP E1 ■ 1 Beisanhuan Zhong Lu ■ 6237 1177 ■ Subway: Olympic Park ■ Open 9:30am–5pm Tue–Sat ■ Adm ■ www.cstm.org.cn

Exhibits begin with ancient science, highlighting China's "technological pre-eminence in history." The technology comes up to date with Chinese space capsules, robots, and an Astro-vision Theater incorporating state-of-the-art cinematography.

10 National Olympic Stadium (Bird's Nest)

Inspired by Chinese ceramics, the design of interlocking steel beams was initially supporting a retractable roof. This was later removed, but what remains is still a stunning structure. Since 2008, the Bird's Nest *(see p44)* has hosted everything from auto-racing and soccer matches to pop concerts and a winter carnival.

GREEN BEIJING

▶ MORNING

Be at the East Gate (Dong Men) of the **Summer Palace** *(see pp28–9)* for 8:30am to beat both the heat (if you are visiting in summer) as well as the crowds. Make your way along the north shore of Kunming Lake via the Long Corridor *(see p28)* and ascend **Longevity Hill** *(see p29)*. Descend again to the Marble Boat and take a pleasure cruiser across the lake to **South Lake Island**. Cross back to the mainland via the supremely elegant **Seventeen-Arch Bridge** *(see p29)*; from here it's a short walk north to exit where you came in at the East Gate. In the car park, pick up a taxi and instruct the driver to take you to **Xiang Shan Park** *(see p99)*, otherwise known as Fragrant Hills Park. Before you enter, **Sculpting In Time** is a café near the East Gate that does good salads, pastas, and pizza.

AFTERNOON

From the park's East Gate, turn right for the **Temple of Brilliance**, built in 1780 and ransacked by Western troops in 1860 and 1900. Close by is the **Liuli Pagoda**, with bells hanging from its eaves that chime in the breeze. Continue north to pass between two small round lakes linked by a small hump-backed bridge – the whole known as the **Spectacles Lakes**. Beyond is a chairlift that takes you up to the top of the "Fragrant Hill." Zigzag back down past many more pavilions to arrive at the **Fragrant Hills Hotel**, designed by Chinese-American architect I. M. Pei, best known for his glass pyramid at the Louvre in Paris and the Suzhou Museum near Shanghai.

See map on pp98–9

TOP10 Farther Afield

Beijing has more than enough sights to keep the average visitor busy. However, after traveling all this way, it would be a shame not to grasp the opportunity to get out of the city. Of course, the Great Wall of China is high on the list for any visitor, but beyond the bustle of Beijing there are also ancient temples nestled on green hillsides and the vast necropolis of the Ming emperors. To the southwest is the 300-year-old stone Marco Polo Bridge and neighboring Wanping, a rare surviving example of a walled city. Both are an easy suburban bus ride from Beijing. Alternatively, most hotels organize tours to these sights.

Imposing statuary at the Ming Tombs

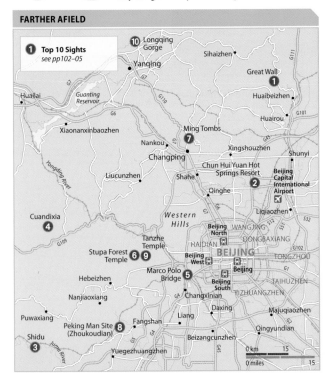

FARTHER AFIELD

1 Top 10 Sights
see pp102–05

10 Longqing Gorge
Sihaizhen
Yanqing
Great Wall 1
Huailai
Guanting Reservoir
Huaibeizhen
Xiaonanxinbaozhen
Huairou
Ming Tombs 7
Nankou
Xingshouzhen
Shunyi
Changping
Chun Hui Yuan Hot Springs Resort 2
Beijing Capital International Airport
Liucunzhen
Shahe
Qinghe
Yongding River
Liqiaozhen
Cuandixia 4
Western Hills
Beijing North
WANGJING
DONGBAXIANG
Tanzhe Temple
HAIDIAN
BEIJING
TONGZHOU
Stupa Forest Temple 6 9
Beijing West
Beijing
TAIHUZHEN
Hebeizhen
Marco Polo Bridge 5
Beijing South
YIZHUANGZHEN
Nanjiaoxiang
Changxinian
Puwaxiang
Peking Man Site (Zhoukoudian) 8
Fangshan
Liang
Daxing
Majuqiaozhen
Shidu 3
Juma River
Beizangcunzhen
Qingyundian
Yuegezhuangzhen

0 km 15
0 miles 15

A stretch of the Great Wall of China surrounded by green hills

1 Great Wall

When in China, a visit to the Great Wall is a must. The closest section to Beijing is at Badaling, and you can get there and back in half a day. However, if you suspect that your appreciation of this matchless monument would be improved by the absence of coach-loads of fellow tourists, then you might want to consider traveling that little bit farther to the sites at Mutianyu, Huanghua Cheng, and Simatai *(see pp34–5)*. This area tends to be fiercely hot in the summer, and bitterly cold in the winter. Go prepared with sunscreen and lots of water on warmer days, and with warm clothing layers on colder ones.

2 Chun Hui Yuan Hot Springs Resort

20 miles (33 km) N of Beijing ▪ 6945 4433 ▪ Bus 942 from Dong Zhi Men to Yu Zhuang, from the stop, turn left and walk just over 1 mile (2 km) to the resort, or take a taxi from Beijing ▪ www.chunhuiyuan.cn

After a day of hiking or rock climbing, unwind at the Chun Hui Yuan Hot Springs Resort. Sink into a hot tub, swim in the pool, try a sauna, or book a spa treatment. Everything here is geared toward total rejuvenation.

3 Shidu

62 miles (100 km) SW of Beijing ▪ 6134 9009 ▪ Bus 917 from Tianqiao station

With its stunning natural scenery, Shidu offers a fabulous escape from the commotion of urban Beijing. In the olden days, travelers had to cross the Juma River ten times to journey through Shidu and nearby Zhangfang village. The name Shidu means "Ten Crossings." Pleasant walking trails wind along the riverbank between impressive gorges and limestone formations. Also located here are four vertigo-inducing glass bridges.

Boating at the gorge in Shidu

The mountainside village of Cuandixia

4 Cuandixia

Near Zhaitang town, 56 miles (90 km) W of Beijing ▪ 6981 9333 ▪ Subway: Pingguo Yuan (1 hr), then taxi, or bus 892 (3 daily, last bus back at 3:35pm) ▪ Adm

On a steep mountainside, Cuandixia is a picturesque hamlet of courtyard houses (siheyuan), most dating from the Ming and Qing dynasties. A ticket allows access to the entire village, which can be explored in a few hours. The population consists of about 29 families. Those wanting an experience of rural hospitality can arrange accommodations with a local family.

5 Marco Polo Bridge

10 miles (16 km) SW of Beijing ▪ 8389 2521 ▪ Subway: Dawayao, then taxi or bus 339 ▪ Open 7am–8pm daily (Nov–Apr: to 6pm)

Straddling the Yongding River near the reconstructed Wanping fortress, this marble bridge, also known as Lugou Bridge, was first built during the Jin dynasty in 1189 but was destroyed by a flood. The current structure dates to 1698, and acquires its name from Marco Polo's description of it in his treatise *The Travels*. The balustrades along the length of the bridge are decorated with over 400 stone lions, each one different from the rest. On July 7, 1937, the Japanese Imperial Army and Nationalist Chinese soldiers exchanged fire here, leading to war and the Japanese occupation of Beijing.

6 Stupa Forest Temple (Talin Si)

28 miles (45 km) W of Beijing ▪ 6086 2505 ▪ Subway: Pingguo Yuan (1 hr), then bus 931 ▪ Open 8am–5pm daily ▪ Adm

Near the parking lot for the Tanzhe Temple is this even more fascinating temple, notable for its collection of brick stupas hidden among the foliage. Every stupa was built in memory of a renowned monk. The towering edifices were built in a variety of designs, and the earliest dates from the Jin dynasty (1115–1234).

7 Ming Tombs

The Ming Tombs (see pp32–3) are the resting place for 13 of the 16 Ming emperors. These are Confucian shrines and follow a standard layout of a main gate leading to a series of courtyards and a main hall, with a "soul tower" and burial mound beyond. The tombs are not as colorful and elaborate as Buddhist and Daoist structures, and only three are open to the public, but the necropolis is a worthwhile stop-off as part of an excursion to the Great Wall.

Bronze statue at the Ming Tombs

Diorama at the Peking Man Site

⑧ Peking Man Site (Zhoukoudian)

30 miles (48 km) SW of Beijing ▪ 6930 1278 ▪ Bus 917 or 836 from Beijing's Tianqiao station to Fangshan, then taxi or bus 38 ▪ Open 8:30am–4:30pm daily ▪ Adm

In the 1920s, archeologists removed from a cave at Zhoukoudian some 40-odd fossilized bones and primitive implements, which they identified as the prehistoric remains of Peking Man. It was thought that this exciting discovery provided the much sought-after link between Neanderthals and modern humans. Designated a UNESCO World Heritage Site, the area is geared toward specialists,

MARCO POLO

Whether Venetian trader and explorer Marco Polo (1254–1324) ever visited China is much disputed. The book he dictated to a ghost writer, who embroidered it substantially, describes aspects of Far Eastern life in much detail, including paper money, the Grand Canal, the structure of a Mongol army, tigers, and the bridge that now bears his name. *The Travels of Marco Polo*, however, may be based on earlier journeys by his father and uncles, and stories from Arab Silk Road merchants.

although the small museum has an interesting collection of tools and bone fragments. Peking Man himself is not here – his remains mysteriously disappeared during World War II.

⑨ Tanzhe Temple

28 miles (45 km) W of Beijing ▪ 6086 2505 ▪ Subway: Pingguo Yuan (1 hr), then bus 931 ▪ Open 8am–5pm daily ▪ Adm

This enormous temple dates back to the 3rd century AD, when it was known as Jiafu Si. It was later renamed for the adjacent mountain, Tanzhe Shan. It has a splendid mountainside setting, and its halls rise up the steep incline. The temple is especially famous for its odd-shaped, ancient trees. Eateries here may be over-priced, so bring your own lunch.

Colorful model of Longqing Gorge

⑩ Longqing Gorge

25 miles (40 km) NW of Beijing ▪ Express bus 919 (5:45am–7pm) from Deshengmen station; get off at Yanqing Dongguan, then take bus Y15 or a taxi to Longqingxia ▪ Open 7:30am–4:30pm daily (during Ice Lantern Festival, Jan & Feb: 9am–10pm daily) ▪ Adm

About 25 miles (40 km) away from the bustle of Beijing, this area boasts lush landscapes. Adventure seekers can go bungee-jumping and zip-lining. Those wanting a more relaxing break can visit the Diamond Temple or go up to the top of the dam using the 846-ft- (258-m-) long Dragon Escalator.

See map on p102 ←

Streetsmart

Red lanterns hanging for the New Year's celebrations at Di Tan Park

Getting To and Around Beijing

Arriving by Air

Until the new Daxing International Airport opens in late 2019, **Beijing Capital Airport** remains the best way to enter and leave the city. There are direct links to countless national and international locations with China's flagship carrier, **Air China**, as well as international lines **China Airlines**, **China Eastern**, and **China Southern**, plus numerous local carriers. It's also worth checking on flights to neighboring Tianjin and traveling to Beijing by the 30 to 40-minute bullet train, which runs every 10 to 15 minutes and costs ¥54.5. Check for flights on **Ctrip** or **Elong**.

A taxi from Capital Airport to central Beijing should be ¥100–150, including the ¥5 toll, depending on your location and traffic. Make sure your driver uses the meter, and have your hotel's name and phone number written in Chinese. It is best to avoid the illegal drivers who approach you at the airport.

A cheaper option, at ¥25, is the **Beijing Airport Express**, a subway line that terminates in Dong Zhi Men. Buy your IC card here, then transfer to city metro, bus, taxi or *san lun che* (pedicab). Six shuttle bus lines also run to various parts of the city, with one night bus service to downtown, and tickets for these cost ¥20 to 30.

Arriving by Sea

Beijing is a landlocked city, but but ferries from Taiwan, South Korea and Japan disembark at **Tianjin Port (Tianjin Xingang),** and you can take a metro, bus or a taxi (around ¥25) to Tanggu Railway Station for the bullet train.

Arriving by Train

China's extensive train network is an excellent way to travel. Newer trains usually ferry business-people back and forth, but the older trains are ideal for families. Bring snacks to share, and you'll enjoy warm, cozy journeys. The hub of the country's travel industry, Beijing offers direct international routes to Ulaanbataar, Moscow, Hanoi and Pyongyang from **Beijing Railway Station** (metro line 2), **South Railway Station** (lines 4 and 14), and **West Railway Station** (lines 7 and 9). **North Railway Station** (also called Xizhimen Station, lines 2, 4 and 13) is for domestic travel. The new **Fengtai Railway Station** (lines 10 and 16) in the south of the city will open in 2020.

Trains come in an alphabet of classes, from G, the highest-level speed train, with business class and soft sleepers, to K, with hard and soft seats, hard and soft sleepers, and deluxe soft sleepers. The hard sleeper is adequate, but avoid the hard seats. Numbered trains are the slowest and have seats only. Stations are signposted in Chinese and English, but arrive at any station one to two hours early to navigate the crowds. Avoid travel during holiday "golden" weeks, May 1 and October 1.

Arriving by Bus

Dong Zhi Men Station (lines 2 and 13, Beijing Airport Express) is Beijing's main bus station, but other stations are scattered around the city and services reach all over China.

Getting Around by Subway

Beijing now has 22 subway lines, with more on the way. The fare varies with distance, but you can get almost anywhere for ¥6 to ¥10. Buy a Beijing IC card from any station for bus (discount) and metro (no discount), and top it up at any counter or machine. The subway is well lit and frequent trains operate from 5am to 11:30pm. A teller at each stop who will sell you a ticket if you point to your intended stop on a subway map. A bus and subway schedule is available online. Signs and announcements are in Chinese and English, but street maps are only in Chinese, so ask for an exit letter. Most venues are metro accessible.

Getting Around by Bus

For non-Chinese speakers, buses are harder to navigate, but show the Chinese address to a friendly passenger, and they'll tell you when to alight. Use cash (fares range between ¥1 to 12 depending on distance), or your IC card to avail a discount of up to 60 per cent. The **Tour Beijing** and **Beijing Trip** websites have prices and other useful information.

Tickets and Transport Cards

Purchase a Beijing IC Card or "Yikatong" inside metro stations, bus stations, and some Chinese supermarkets for a ¥100 and ¥20 deposit respectively, then top it up as needed. It can be used for the metro, buses, taxis and "S" trains to the Great Wall, and unused money can be refunded.

Getting Around by Taxi

Although cabs are comparatively affordable, many Beijing taxi drivers lack city knowledge, or see foreigners as easy marks. Never take an unmetered taxi, and avoid parked cars outside tourist attractions; flag one down instead. Black (illegal) cabs are regular cars marked with a horizontal red windshield light; these are not reliable for price or safety. Uber and Lyft are difficult unless you read Chinese. Make sure you have the destination written in Chinese, and a phone number to call. Note that taxis don't accept credit cards.

Getting Around by Bicycle

Cycling is the ideal way to see Beijing, particularly the *hutongs* and historical areas. You can borrow a bike from most hostels or rent one from organizations such as **Bike Beijing**. Using public bikes, such as Mobike, involves downloading an app and a registration process, but it's a good way to save money as bikes cost just ¥1 per hour. Payment for these is only via WeChat or Alipay.

Inexperienced cyclists should take care: e-bike riders and cyclists don't tend to stop at red lights, and they frequently drive and ride on the wrong side of the road. There are bike lanes everywhere, but cars use them as parking lots, which forces the riders into the streets. Neither cyclists nor pedestrians look both ways before pulling out or stepping into the road, and zebra crossings are nothing more than asphalt decoration. It's best to try a day or so in the quieter *hutongs* to gauge your comfort level. Once you're out in the city traffic, being a proactive, defensive rider is the best course of action.

DIRECTORY

ARRIVING BY AIR

Air China
📞 4008 100 999
🌐 airchina.com.cn

Beijing Airport Express
🌐 en.bcia.com.cn/traffic/express

Beijing Capital Airport
🌐 en.bcia.com.cn

China Airlines
📞 400 888 6998
🌐 china-airlines.com

China Eastern
📞 95530
🌐 en.ceair.com

China Southern
📞 4006 695 539
🌐 csair.com/en/index.shtml

Ctrip
🌐 ctrip.com

Elong
🌐 elong.net

ARRIVING BY SEA

Tianjin Port (Tianjin Xingang)
📞 (22) 2570 7550
🌐 ptacn.com

ARRIVING BY TRAIN

Beijing Railway Station
📞 5101 9999

North Railway Station
📞 5186 6233

South Railway Station
📞 5183 6272

West Railway Station
📞 5182 4233

ARRIVING BY BUS

Dongzhimen Station
📞 6467 1346

GETTING AROUND BY SUBWAY

Bus and Subway Schedule
🌐 travelchinaguide.com/cityguides/beijing/transportation

GETTING AROUND BY BUS

Beijing Trip
🌐 beijingtrip.com

Tour Beijing
🌐 tour-beijing.com/public_bus

GETTING AROUND BY BICYCLE

Bike Beijing
🌐 bikebeijing.com
📞 0652 65857

Mobike
🌐 mobike.com

Practical Information

Passports and Visas

Visa requirements are increasingly stringent. Travelers should have six months' validity on their passports and allow at least one month for the application process. Prepare to pay $45–200, depending on country. Visitors also need to be in possession of a return plane ticket and an accommodation itinerary so if you're visiting friends, book a hostel and cancel later. China offers many countries' citizens a 144-hour transit visa, provided they have an international round-trip ticket. Single-entry visas are valid for three months, double-entry for six months, and multiple-entry for six, 12, or 24 months. It's a good idea to carry your passport everywhere; you will need it to purchase tickets and change money. If you need consular assistance, **Australia, Canada, the United Kingdom,** and the **United States** all have embassies in Beijing. You will also need your passport for entry into all museums in Beijing, including the Forbidden City.

Customs and Immigration

Few people are searched upon leaving or entering Beijing, but all bags go through a scanner. At politically sensitive times, books may be examined, and anti-China material will be confiscated. Food, two bottles of liquor, and two cartons of cigarettes can avoid duty, while any personal-use electronics brought into the country must be taken out again. If you are carrying ¥20,000 (or any currency worth $5,000), you must declare it. Antiquities, recreational drugs, protected-species products, and weapons are strictly prohibited; even souvenir knives are confiscated from checked luggage. China has zero drug tolerance; to be safe, bring your physician's prescription with you. The Chinese government has a useful website outlining customs regulations.

Travel Safety Advice

For the latest travel safety advice, check the websites of the **UK Foreign and Commonwealth Office,** the **Australian Department of Foreign Affairs and Trade,** and the **US Department of State.**

Travel Insurance

Travel insurance is vital. Medical care at foreign hospitals costs US-level prices. Most local Chinese hospitals will not take insurance and will require a hefty deposit for more expensive procedures.

Health

Although China doesn't require vaccinations, those spending months traveling around the country should consider the basics. International-standard facilities – such as **Beijing United Family Hospital, International SOS,** and **Hong Kong International Medical Clinic** – have English-speaking doctors, but when visiting Chinese hospitals – even **Peking Union Medical College Hospital**'s international department – you may need an interpreter. (Be sure to mention medications, allergies, and family history – not everyone asks.) Pharmacies sell both Western and traditional Chinese medicine. The **International SOS pharmacy** is ideal for buying over-the-counter medicine and getting advice in English; however contact an international hospital for emergencies.

Those concerned about pollution can download an app for hourly reports. Buy a 2.5PM mask and plan indoor activities for bad days. It is safe to brush your teeth with tap water, but always drink bottled water. Western digestive systems can struggle with the oil in Chinese food, so it's a good idea to bring anti-diarrhea medicine.

Personal Security

Beijing is surprisingly safe, but watch your wallet on public transport. Sanlitun's increased police presence has made this once-sketchy area significantly safer. However, scams are rife; look out for the "art students" in Wangfujing who want to practice their English and sell you paintings, or the locals in Tian'an Men Square who invite you to a teahouse – you may be stuck with a $600 bill. Solo female travelers should choose official taxis and a female pedicab driver – and always stay awake.

Emergency Services

There are English lines available for emergencies, such as the **Foreign Emergency Services** as well as the ambulance number, but to save time, ask a local to make the call. However, it can be quicker to take a taxi for going to the hospital, rather than waiting for an ambulance.

Currency and Banking

The national currency is the *yuan* (¥), also known as *renminbi* or *kuai* (slang). Notes come in ¥1, ¥5, ¥10, ¥20, ¥50, and ¥100 and 1 and 5 *jiao* (slang: *mao*); coins come in 1 and 5 *jiao*, and ¥1. Most banks have 24-hour ATMs that take both international and domestic cards,

as well as international credit cards. To change money, try major banks.

Telephone and Internet

Free Wi-Fi is available at most restaurants and cafés; high-end hotels often charge a room-usage fee, but keep public areas open. You'll need a VPN to access Facebook, Google, and most Western sites. The most popular ones are Hide.me, ExpressVPN and PandaPow, but this situation is fluid, so check reviews before leaving and sign up for free trials. Apple and Google maps should work with a VPN, or try **Ulmon** or **Baidu**. WeChat offers free audio and video calls and messaging to local and international users.

The best network provider is China Unicom. Purchase a SIM card at the airport or at local shops (you will require a passport), and test it before you go; call 10100 and wait for the prompt to activate international calling – and ask for discount numbers for international calls. You can buy top-ups from phone shops or via WeChat. Make sure your phone will work in China; GSM phones should have 900 and 1800 Mhz frequencies or bands.

Postal Services

Open 9am–5pm daily, **China Post** has several branches in Beijing, but couriers are usually faster. For next-day deliveries within the city, ask your hotel to arrange a *kuadi* – which costs around ¥30.

DIRECTORY

PASSPORTS AND VISAS

Australian Embassy
📞 5140 4111
🌐 china.embassy.gov.au

British Embassy
📞 5192 4000
🌐 gov.uk/world/organisations/british-embassy-beijing

Canadian Embassy
📞 5139 4000
🌐 beijing.gc.ca

United States Embassy
📞 8531 3000
🌐 china.usembassy-china.org.cn

CUSTOMS AND IMMIGRATION

General Administration of Customs PRC
🌐 english.customs.gov.cn

TRAVEL SAFETY ADVICE

Australian Department of Foreign Affairs and Trade
🌐 smartraveller.gov.au
🌐 dfat.gov.au/travel

UK Foreign and Commonwealth Office
🌐 gov.uk/foreign-travel-advice/china

US Department of State
🌐 travel.state.gov

HEALTH

Beijing United Family Hospital
🌐 beijing.ufh.com.cn
📞 5927 7120

Hong Kong International Medical Clinic, Beijing
🌐 hkclinic.com
📞 6553 2288 (24 hours)

International SOS
📞 6462 9100
🌐 internationalsos.com

Peking Union Medical College Hospital
📞 6915 6699
🌐 pumch.cn

EMERGENCY SERVICES

Ambulance
📞 120

Foreign Emergency Services
📞 6462 9100

Police
📞 110

TELEPHONE AND INTERNET

Baidu
🌐 baidu.com

Ulmon
🌐 ulmon.com

POSTAL SERVICES

China Post
🌐 english.chinapost.com.cn

Opening Hours

Restaurants are usually open 10am–10pm, but Chinese restaurants often close 2–5pm, except for the 24-hour options on Gui Jie. Many bars serve snacks until 11pm, and convenience stores and street food are always available. Shops, stores, and supermarkets usually stay open 9am–9pm, while banks, post offices, and pharmacies operate 9am–5pm. Museums and attractions are usually open 9am–4:30pm, but some have shorter winter hours, and nearly all are closed on Mondays. For distant or unusual attractions, it is always best to call ahead to confirm opening hours.

Time Difference

Beijing is eight hours ahead of GMT, 13 hours ahead of New York, and two hours behind Sydney. The city does not use Daylight Saving Time.

Electrical Appliances

Electrical current is 220 volts AC, so North Americans should use dual-voltage appliances or a converter. China uses two parallel flat pins, two parallel round pins, or two or three slanted flat pins – and some sockets accept all of these. Buying a universal adapter is advisable.

Press

China Daily and *Global Times* are the best choices for English-language news; try also **Xinhua**, online. For entertainment, the expats are *Time Out Beijing*, *That's Beijing*, and *The Beijinger*. For English-language radio and television, try *CRI (China Radio International)*, and *CCTV9* for documentaries and news. CCTV also has channels in Spanish, Russian, French, and Arabic. Big hotels sell magazines such as *Time* and *The Economist*, and offer CCTV, BBC, HBO, and Hong Kong cable.

Driving

Foreigners holding a visa valid for 90 days or more can apply for a China Provisional Driving Permit at **Beijing Capital Airport**'s Terminal Three; there are usually some English speakers there who can help with the paperwork. However, this license is only valid for rental cars within Beijing, and most rental agencies don't always rent to foreigners. Beijing has heavy traffic but excellent public transportation, and hiring a local car with a driver is a more viable option.

Weather

Temperate weather makes both spring and autumn the ideal seasons to visit the city. During summer, temperatures range from 80° F (27° C) to a soaring 105° F (41° C), while winter can be anywhere from 26° F (-3° C) to 16° F (-9° C). Beijing generally has a dry climate, but summer sees frequent rain as well as some hailstorms, while winter tends to have the heaviest pollution.

Travelers with Specific Needs

Since hosting the 2008 Olympics, Beijing has increased the number of barrier-free facilities. These include most attractions (and parts of the Great Wall), subways, and many buses; there are also wheelchair-friendly taxis available to order. Most shop and hotel entrances will have ramps, and most hotels will have lifts.

Visitor Information

There are tourist offices in each airport terminal and around the city.

Trips and Tours

Travel China Guide, **China Highlights**, and **Discover Beijing Tours** offer standard packages and day trips. Or try **Bespoke Travel Company**'s customized tours. **Private car and van drivers** can make budget trips to the Great Wall.

Smoking and Etiquette

Smoking is banned in indoor public spaces. The legal age for drinking and smoking is 18 but rarely enforced. Be warned: cheap alcohol is usually fake and often hazardous.

Shopping

The famed fake-goods open markets are disappearing; now Beijing boasts foreign brands from Apple to Zara. Also mushrooming are chic boutiques, particularly in the areas of Gulou and

Sanlitun (see p89), which has the **Taikoo Li** outdoor mall and some of the city's best shops and restaurants. Other good shopping areas include Wangfujing (see pp70–71) in the city center and Parkview Green (see p92) in Chaoyang district. If you can't go without haggling, visit Panjiayuan Market for antiques, and the Silk Market for bags (see p61). Traditional craft shops are best found in Gulou, and you can't beat Nan Luogu Xiang (see p81) for quirky souvenirs. Buy art supplies at Liulichang (see p75), and reading material at **The Bookworm** in Sanlitun or the **Wangfujing Foreign Language Bookstore**.

Foreign visitors can get VAT rebates on purchases worth more than ¥500 (spent in a single store on a single day) on a stay of less than 90 days; show your passport and your receipt, and take the gifts with you on the plane.

Where to Eat

The complexity of China's eight major cuisines (and thousands of subsets) is staggering. Guangdong is famous for its dim sum and chicken's feet. Sichuan and Hunan are the spiciest cuisines, but Sichuan uses more oil and peppercorns. Landlocked Anhui stews mountain herbs and vegetables; Fujian, Jiangsu, and Zhejiang focus on seafood. The most foreign-friendly cuisine is Yunnan.

Most restaurants have a vast array of vegetables and tofu dishes, but there are also many dedicated vegetarian restaurants. Rice comes at the meal's end; avoid sticking your chopsticks in the bowl, since it resembles the incense used for funerals.

Most menus have glossy photos, if not English translations. It's a good idea to learn a few key food phrases ("something

with beef/chicken," or "something spicy") and let the kitchen surprise you.

Chinese people eat together. Meals are social affairs and the host pays the check. Tipping is not expected – and often the service reflects that.

Accommodation

For short stays, pick traditional and charming parts of the city; most hostels and courtyard hotels are located in hutongs, which provide food, entertainment, and hours of people-watching. They may also have cafés or rooftop bars, and even hostels can help you arrange tours or drivers. Business hotels are scattered around the city, especially in Chaoyang and the CBD. You can expect good service and excellent English, plus restaurants, a pool, a gym, and a complimentary fruit platter in the room.

DIRECTORY

PRESS

The Beijinger
🖵 thebeijinger.com

CCTV9
🖵 english.cctv.com

China Daily
🖵 chinadaily.com.cn

CRI (China Radio International)
🖵 chinaplus.cri.cn

Global Times
🖵 globaltimes.cn

That's Beijing
🖵 thatsmags.com/beijing

Time Out Beijing
🖵 timeoutbeijing.com

Xinhua
🖵 xinhuanet.com

DRIVING

Beijing Capital Airport
🖵 en.bcia.com.cn

TRIPS AND TOURS

Bespoke Travel Company
📞 151 0167 9082
🖵 bespoketravel company.com

China Highlights
📞 773 283 1999
🖵 chinahighlights.com

Discover Beijing Tours
📞 135 2206 9857
🖵 discoverbeijing tours.com

Private Car and Van Drivers
Mr. Ding
📞 139 1072 8962

Mr. Jack
📞 136 5137 4172
Mr. Li
📞 136 2112 7407

Travel China Guide
📞 29 8523 6688
🖵 travelchinaguide.com

SHOPPING

The Bookworm
📞 6503 2050
🖵 beijingbookworm.com

Taikoo Li
📞 6417 6110
🖵 taikoolisanlitun.com

Wangfujing Foreign Language Bookstore
235 Wangfujing St, Dongcheng
📞 6512 6903

Places to Stay

PRICE CATEGORIES

Prices are based on a double room per night (with breakfast if included), with taxes and extra charges.

¥ under ¥400, ¥¥ ¥400–¥1,400, ¥¥¥ over ¥1,400

Luxury and Boutique Hotels

Brickyard

MAP H5 ▪ Beigou Village, near Mutianyu, Great Wall, Huairou ▪ 6162 6506 ▪ brickyard atmutianyu.com ▪ ¥¥
Beijing expats' first choice for romantic getaways, girls' weekends, and even weddings, the Brickyard features some impressive floor-to-ceiling windows, utterly breathtaking views, and beautiful gardens. Enjoy excellent meals made from locally sourced ingredients, and bring your swimsuit to take full advantage of the popular outdoor Jacuzzi.

New World Beijing

MAP F5 ▪ 8 Qinian Jie ▪ 5960 8888 ▪ Subway: Chongwenmen ▪ beijing. newworldhotels.com ▪ ¥¥
Well-located between the Temple of Heaven and Wangfujing, this hotel offers comfortable and smart rooms, a Jacuzzi and a swimming pool. It also has two Chinese restaurants, a tearoom, and a rooftop bar.

Red Wall Garden Hotel

MAP N3 ▪ 41 Shijia Hutong, Dongcheng District ▪ 5169 2222 ▪ www.redwallgarden hotel.com ▪ ¥¥
Sometimes one must sacrifice comfort for tradition. Not so with Red Wall Garden, a luxury boutique hotel that gives you all the romance of the traditional Beijing *hutongs* and their pretty courtyards without the hard mattresses, and with soundproofed rooms.

Shadow Art Puppet Hotel

MAP D2 ▪ 24 Songshu Street, Xicheng District ▪ 8328 7847 ▪ www. shadowartboutique.com ▪ ¥¥
In addition to three weekly puppet shows, this themed hotel in historic Shichahai also offers some free calligraphy, puppet-painting and dumpling-making classes, plus free access to bikes. Hou Hai is only minutes away.

Aman at the Summer Palace

MAP G6 ▪ 1 Gong Men Qian Jie ▪ 5987 9999 ▪ www.amanresorts.com ▪ ¥¥¥
Guests at this stunning hotel 6 miles (10 km) northwest of the city center enjoy private access to the Summer Palace *(see pp28–9)*, as well as a cinema, stylish spa, and subterranean swimming pool.

China World Summit Wing

MAP H4 ▪ 1 Jianguo Men Wai Dajie ▪ 6505 2299 ▪ Subway: Guomao ▪ www.shangri-la.com/ beijing ▪ ¥¥¥
This hotel in Beijing's second-tallest tower affords stunning city views from its swish Atmosphere bar on the 80th floor. There are also four restaurants, a spa, and an infinity pool.

Eclat Beijing

MAP H3 ▪ 9 Dongdaqiao Lu, Chaoyang District ▪ 8561 2888 ▪ www.eclat hotels.com/beijing ▪ ¥¥¥
A stylishly designed boutique hotel with an impressive art collection in the public spaces, Eclat Beijing also has the capital's first pool suites. It offers a 24-hour food lounge, plus other facilities such as a personal butler service.

Hotel Côte Cour

MAP F3 ▪ 70 Yanyue Hutong ▪ 6523 9598 ▪ Subway: Dongsi ▪ www. hotelcotecourbj.com ▪ ¥¥¥
Hidden away amid a maze of local *hutongs*, this comfortable boutique hotel presents a modern take on a traditional *siheyuan* courtyard house. It has stylish fittings and under-floor heating that is very welcome in winter.

NUO Hotel

MAP H6 ▪ 2 Jiangtai Road, Chaoyang District ▪ 5926 8888 ▪ www. nuohotel.com ▪ ¥¥¥
China's groundbreaking foray into the luxury market, NUO is the first among a planned group of 15 hotels in various global capitals. Contemporary art superstar Zeng Fanzhi, who served as a consultant, installed his own original art, building a theme for the hotel's 798 Art District location.

The Opposite House
MAP H2 ■ 11 Sanlitun Road ■ 6417 6688 ■ Subway: Tuanjiehu ■ www.theopposite house.com ■ ¥¥¥
Designed by renowned Japanese architect Kengo Kuma, The Opposite House is part of Taikoo Li Sanlitun. The 99 spacious rooms, all with natural wooden floors and deep oak soaking tubs, are a design experience, as is the stainless-steel pool.

Park Hyatt Beijing
MAP H4 ■ 2 Jianguo Men Dajie ■ 8567 1234 ■ Subway: Guomao ■ www.hyatt.com ■ ¥¥¥
High-end service and style are the watchwords at the Park Hyatt hotel. Chic, contemporary accommodations, coupled with stylish bars and restaurants, draw the most discerning of local and international clients.

The Peninsula Beijing
MAP N4 ■ 8 Jinyu Hutong ■ 8516 2888 ■ Subway: Dengshikou ■ www.peninsula.com ■ ¥¥¥
The luxurious rooms here have plasma TVs; even the marble bathrooms have a small screen. Two terrific restaurants (Huang Ting and Jing), a recent restyling, excellent service, and a central location make this one of the city's best accommodation choices.

Waldorf
MAP N4 ■ 5-15 Jinyu Hutong, off Wangfujing Street, Dongcheng District ■ 8520 8989 ■ www.waldorfastoria3.hilton.com ■ ¥¥¥
This is the jewel of downtown Beijing. Guests rave about the creative design, contemporary art display, prime location, and excellent service. For an ultra luxurious China experience, book the premium Hutong Villa, which boasts a private swimming pool.

Courtyard Hotels

Red Lantern House
MAP D2 ■ 5 Zheng Jue Hutong, Xinjiekou Nan Dajie, Xicheng ■ 8328 3935 ■ Subway: Jishuitan ■ www.redlanternhouse.com ■ ¥
The family-owned Red Lantern House occupies a main building and two pretty courtyards. It is only a stone's throw away from the lively bars of Hou Hai.

Bamboo Garden Hotel
MAP E1 ■ 24 Xiao Shi Qiao Hutong ■ 5852 0088 ■ Subway: Gulou Dajie ■ www.bbgh.com.cn ■ ¥¥
Close to Hou Hai lake, this is the oldest of Beijing's traditional hotels, with the largest and probably most elaborate courtyards, plus beautiful rockeries and covered pathways.

Double Happiness
MAP E2 ■ 37 Dongsisitiao, Dongcheng District ■ 6400 7762 ■ Subway: Dongsi ■ www.double happinesscourtyard hotel.com ■ ¥¥
A hotel with a great ambience, Double Happiness has small rooms with traditional decor but modern bathrooms. There are lovely little courtyards outside the rooms along with a pleasant patio.

Duge Courtyard Hotel
MAP E2 ■ 26 Qianyuanensi Hutong, Nan Luogu Xiang ■ 6445 7463 ■ Subway: Anding Men ■ www.dugehotel.com ■ ¥¥
The Duge Courtyard's 7 individually decorated suites are designed in a dramatic and decadent fashion, and hidden away behind two imposing doors. The Peony Pavilion room is pretty and classic, while other rooms have a more contemporary vibe. All are centered on one of several small courtyards.

Fly by Knight Courtyard
MAP F3 ■ 6 Dengcao Hutong, Dongcheng ■ 6559 7966 ■ www.flybyknightbeijing.com ■ ¥¥
One of the best-value *hutong* guesthouses, this friendly, clean and well run ex-hostel has spacious and comfortable traditional rooms, as well as an excellent English-speaking staff. The kung fu classes organized in the hotel courtyard add to the authentic atmosphere.

Kelly's Courtyard
MAP C3 ■ 25 Xiaoyuan Hutong, off Bingmasi Hutong, Xisi South Street ■ 6611 8515 ■ Subway: Xisi ■ Bus: 47, 105, 690, or 808 ■ www.kellyscourtyard.com ■ ¥¥
A stylish and modernized hideaway in a historic *hutong* near Xidan and the financial district, this hostel is owned by a travel-loving Chinese fashion designer.

The Orchid
MAP E2 ▪ 65 Baochao Hutong, Dongcheng District ▪ 8565 9295 ▪ ¥¥
Tucked away down a quiet *hutong* in the hippest, chicest part of Beijing's Old City, The Orchid features white-washed, airy rooms with polished hardwood floors, plus an excellent break-fast. The atmospheric terrace restaurant offers a range of Chinese, South Asian, as well as Middle Eastern meals, and serves sundowners all day long.

Business Hotels

East
22 Jiuxianqiao Rd, Chaoyang ▪ 8426 0888 ▪ www.east-beijing.com ▪ ¥¥
Set amid parkland in the INDIGO business district, this contemporary hotel caters to the high-end business traveler. All 369 rooms and 23 executive suites have amenities including an LCD TV, free Wi-Fi, Bose audio system and rainfall showers in the bathroom. The hotel also has two good restau-rants, a swimming pool, and gym facilities.

Park Plaza Hotel
MAP N3 ▪ 97 Jinbao Jie ▪ 8522 1999 ▪ Subway: Wangfujing ▪ www.parkplaza.com/beijingcn ▪ ¥¥
The stylish Park Plaza is a peaceful oasis in one of the city's fastest-devel-oping precincts. Guest rooms feature stylish designer touches, and the hotel is conveniently located for both the Forbidden City and Wangfujing Dajie.

Four Seasons Beijing
MAP H1 ▪ 48 Liang Ma Qiao Lu ▪ 5695 8888 ▪ www.fourseasons.com/beijing ▪ ¥¥¥
Exemplary service and premium amenities await business and leisure travelers who stay at this impressive modern hotel. The interiors are artistic, and the hotel also has two signature restaurants, a deluxe spa, and a popular lounge bar.

Hilton Beijing Wangfujing
MAP M4 ▪ 8 Wangfujing Dong Dajie ▪ 5812 8888 ▪ Subway: Wangfujing ▪ www.hilton.com ▪ ¥¥¥
Spacious, open-plan rooms, warm service, and a large swimming pool are just some of the draws at this hotel. A central location within walking distance of Tian'an Men Square and the Forbidden City is another key feature.

Kerry Center Hotel
MAP H4 ▪ 1 Guanghua Lu ▪ 6561 8833 ▪ Subway: Guomao ▪ www.shangri-la.com ▪ ¥¥¥
The Kerry Center Hotel combines the Shangri-La group's high service standards with bright, modern room design. The Kerry is also home to the Centro cocktail bar *(see p59)* and extensive health facilities.

Langham Place
MAP H5 ▪ 1 Yi Jing Rd, opposite Terminal 3 ▪ 6457 5555 ▪ Subway: Beijing International Airport ▪ www.langhamhotels.com ▪ ¥¥¥
Located near Beijing Capital Airport, Langham Place offers luxury rooms

and suites, as well as several modern restau-rants and bars, a club lounge, gym, free Wi-Fi and an art gallery. There is also a free airport shuttle bus service.

The Ritz-Carlton, Beijing
MAP H6 ▪ 83A Jianguo Lu, China Central Place, Chaoyang District ▪ 5908 8888 ▪ Subway: Dawanglu ▪ www.ritzcarlton.com ▪ ¥¥¥
A perfect retreat for both business and leisure travelers, this 305-room deluxe hotel offers fine dining, excellent facilities for meetings and events, and a high-end spa.

The Westin Beijing Chaoyang
MAP H1 ▪ Bei San Huan Dajie ▪ 5922 8888 ▪ Subway: Liangma Qiao ▪ www.marriott.com ▪ ¥¥¥
Outstanding service is complemented by stylish decor here. Being set on a ring road is not ideal, but the main sights and shopping areas are only a short taxi ride away.

Mid-Range Hotels

Red Hotel
MAP G2 ▪ 10 Taiping Zhuang Chunxiu Lu ▪ 6417 1066 ▪ Subway: Dong Shi Men ▪ www.red-hotel.com ▪ ¥
Staying true to its name, the former Red House Hotel stands out with its vibrant facade. This establishment offers clean, cheerful rooms, which are good value for money. There's a popular soccer bar on the premises, and it's a short walk to more bars in the Sanlitun District.

Crystal Orange
MAP G4 ▪ 25 Yonganli Zhong Jie, Chaoyang ▪ 6566 1515 ▪ Subway: Yonganli ▪ ¥¥
This good-value hotel is furnished in bold colors, with Andy Warhol prints adorning the walls of the lobby. Comfortable rooms have spacious bathrooms and feature all modern conveniences, including Wi-Fi and iPod docks.

Hade Men Hotel
MAP N6 ▪ 2A Chongwen Men Wai Dajie ▪ 400 838 1766 ▪ Subway: Chongwen Men ▪ ¥¥
The Hade Men is among the older hotels in Beijing, but it's been renovated to a good standard for this price range. Rooms are comfortable, if a bit gaudy, with pleasant views from the upper floors. It is around the corner from the railway station.

Holiday Inn Express Dong Zhi Men
MAP G2 ▪ 1 Chunxiu Lu, Dongcheng ▪ 6416 9999 ▪ Subway: Dong Zhi Men ▪ www.hiexpress.com ▪ ¥¥
Centrally located between Dong Zhi Men and Gongti Bei Lu, with easy access to the city's main attractions, this hotel offers rooms at affordable prices. A good breakfast is included in the room rate, as is Wi-Fi.

Motel 268
MAP N4 ▪ 19 Jin Yu Hutong ▪ 5167 1666 ▪ Subway: Dengshikou ▪ ¥¥
Because of its prime location, this branch of China's economy hotel chain Motel 168 has been branded Motel 268. The 156-room property offers

doubles and family rooms, all with Wi-Fi, air-conditioning, and a television. Be sure to ask for a room with a window.

Penta Beijing
MAP F5 ▪ 3–18 Chongwen Men Wai Daije, Dongcheng ▪ 6708 1188 ▪ Subway: Beijing Railway Station ▪ www.pentahotels.com ▪ ¥¥
Located close to Tian'an Men Square and the Temple of Heaven, this stylish hotel is suited to those traveling for business and leisure. As well as good and modern in-room facilities, it offers a lounge, gym, games area, and free Wi-Fi.

Budget Hotels

Downtown Backpackers
MAP E2 ▪ 85 Nan Luo Gu Xiang ▪ 8400 2429 ▪ Subway: Nan Luogu Xiang ▪ www.backpackingchina.com ▪ ¥
A good-value option in the heart of one of Beijing's most vibrant *hutongs*. This hostel is also minutes from the lakes as well as myriad restaurants and bars. It offers clean single rooms, doubles with attached bath, and 6–8 bed dorms.

Leo Hostel
MAP L6 ▪ 52 Dazhalan Xijie ▪ 6303 0879 ▪ Subway: Qian Men ▪ www.leohostel.com ▪ ¥
Leo Hostel benefits from an excellent location south of Tian'an Men Square, in among old lanes. Rooms range from four to ten-bed dorms to doubles. Facilities include free Wi-Fi, computer with

internet connection, a pool table and a second-hand book exchange.

Saga International Youth Hostel
MAP N3 ▪ 9 Shijia Hutong ▪ 6527 2773 ▪ Subway: Dengshikou ▪ www.sagayouthhostelbeijing.cn ▪ ¥
Featuring spotless doubles, triples, and dorm rooms, plus a communal kitchen and café and a shaded courtyard, this hostel has helpful English-speaking staff who will organize ticket bookings and tours.

Templeside Deluxe Hutong House Hostel
MAP C3 ▪ 2 An Ping Xiang, Zhao Deng Yu Lu ▪ 6617 2571 ▪ Subway: Fucheng Men ▪ www.templeside.com ▪ ¥
This courtyard hostel gives budget travelers a glimpse into traditional Beijing life. It has spacious single, double and family-friendly bunk bedrooms, and a pleasant courtyard garden. Breakfast is served upon request.

The Peking International Youth Hostel
MAP E2 ▪ 113-2 Nan Luogu Xiang, Dongcheng District ▪ 6401 3961/ 8403 9098 ▪ ¥¥
Owned by a local flower designer, this popular hostel exudes shabby-chic decor and has an outdoor courtyard – the latter, a rare budget treat. The restaurant, while comparatively pricey, rates high, and helpful staff will arrange show tickets and day trips for you. The bustling local neighborhood is a favorite with Beijingers.

For a key to hotel price categories see p114

General Index

Acknowledgments

Author
Andrew Humphreys is a travel journalist and writer who spent six months in China launching Time Out Beijing. It is his opinion that Beijing is one of the best cities in the world for food.

Publishing Director Georgina Dee

Publisher Vivien Antwi

Design Director Phil Ormerod

Editorial Ankita Awasthi Tröger, Rachel Fox, Maresa Manara, Sands Publishing Solutions, Anuroop Sanwalia, Sally Schafer, Penny Walker

Cover Design Maxine Pedliham, Vinita Venugopal

Design Hansa Babra, Tessa Bindloss, Sunita Gahir, Rahul Kumar

Picture Research Taiyaba Khatoon, Sumita Khatwani, Ellen Root

Cartography Zafar ul Islam Khan, Suresh Kumar, James MacDonald, Casper Morris

DTP Jason Little, Azeem Siddiqui

Production Igrain Roberts

Factchecker David Leffman

Proofreader Kathryn Glendenning

Indexer Helen Peters

Revisions Dipika Dasgupta, Shikha Kulkarni, Arushi Mathur, Bandana Paul, Priyanka Thakur, Stuti Tiwari, Charles Young

Commissioned Photography Chen Chao

Picture Credits
The publisher would like to thank the following for their kind permission to reproduce their photographs:
Key: a-above; b-below/bottom; c-centre; f-far; l-left; r-right; t-top

123RF.com: Brian Kinney 4t, 16-7.

4Corners: Günter Gräfenhain 4cra; HP Huber 17cr; SIME / Tull & Bruno Morandi 35bl.

Alamy Stock Photo: age fotostock 14cla, / Yuen Man Cheung 30-1c, Sara Janini 30clb; avadaRM 17crb; Sergio Azenha 53cl; Mathias Beinling 72b; Blue Jean Images 49cr, 52tl; Jon Bower China 11bl; Robert Burch 89tl; China Images 27bl; China Photos 95tr; EPA 18cl; epa european pressphoto agency b.v. 46cl, 65br; Dmitry Erokhin 69tr; F1online digitale Bildagentur GmbH 96c; Wayne Farrell 64c; Kevin Foy 90cl; Victor Fraile 44cl; Jan Fritz 29tl; David Gee 3 15tc; Manfred Gottschalk 62c; 70cla; Tim Graham 33tr; Hemis 53tr, 90-1; Henry Westheim Photography 4clb, 33bl; jeremy sutton-hibbert 105tl; Kate Hockenhull 83tl; Iconotec 91cl; imageBROKER 71cl, 104br; jejim120 12br; JLImages 65clb;

John Warburton-Lee Photography 26cla, 105cr; Patric Jonsson 82b; Michael Kemp 25cr; kpzfoto 81br; Keith Levit 61b; Sean Pavone 2tl, 3tl, 8-9, 66-7, 86-7; Wiliam Perry 76tr; Prisma Bildagentur AG 82c; Dirk Renckhoff 11tc, 54cl; REUTERS 64t, 75br; robertharding 43crb, 46b; RosalreneBetancourt 10 73cl; Hans-Joachim Schneider 39tr; Felix Stensson 99br; Keren Su / China Span 34clb; SuperStock 92cla; Ulana Switucha 27tl; TAO Images Limited 32cl, 43bl, 52c, 94tl, / Ren Shulin 30br; Lucas Vallecillos 32-3c; Lucas Vallecillos 25tc; Steve Vidler 12cl, 15cl, 60tl; View Stock 51br; Viewstock 41t; John Woods 11cl; Xinhua 51cl.

AWL Images: Christian Kober 3tr, 106-7; Maurizio Rellini 1; Travel Pix Collection 28bl.

Cai Yi Xuan: Ken Seet 57bl.

Captial Spirits Bar: 84tl.

Courtesy Ullens Center for Contemporary Art: 31cr.

Dreamstime.com: 06photo 10ca; Aakahunaa 40c; Kyle Allen 13tl; Leonid Andronov 13br; 80ca; Beijing Hetuchuangyi Images Co. Ltd. 46tc; Bertrandb 68clb; Caoerlei 34-5; Chinaview 54tr; Chucky 78c; Chuyu 95br; Dk88888 10crb; 63br; Elena Elisseeva 58c; Julie Feinstein 58bl; Fotokon 21tl, 57tr; Frenta 98c; Igor Groshev 35cr; Hungchungchih 7tr; Icara 11cra; Attila Jandi 74cl; Mike K 63tl; Klodien 102tl; Leonidfeng 70b; Peng Li 79b; Yong hian Lim 76b; Linqong 45tr; Luoxubin 45bl; Mengtianhan 2tr, 36-7; Miragik 55cl; Angela Ostafichuk 100t; Sean Pavone 4b,18-9; William Perry 99tl; Ppy2010ha 54bl; Qin0377 10cl; Mario Savoia 55br; Yanhui Song 95t; Sutsaiy 85bc; Libo Tang 50t; Telnyawka 21cr; Winghoong Thong 4cla; Tiffanychan 44t; Vincentstthomas 21br; Vitalyedush 7bl, 10bl, 19br, 20-1, 40tl; Zheng Xiaoqiao 103br; Yuri Yavnik 103t; Xi Zhang 4cl, 75tl, 89b; Zhaohui 52b; Zhiwei Zhou 22-3; Vladimir Zhuravlev 10cr; Zjm7100 27cr, 48tl, 61tl, 68tl, 101cl.

The Georg: 56clb.

Getty Images: Getty Images: AFP 49tl, / Stephen Shaver 14b, / STR 64br; AGF 24bl; China Photos 48b; De Agostini / W. Buss 28-9; DEA Picture Library 38b; DuKai photographer 88tl; Manfred Gottschalk 78tl; Hulton Fine Art Collection 38tc; Gamma-Keystone 39cl; Christian Kober 100clb; Keith Levit 50bl; Luis Castaneda Inc. 4crb, 16bl, 96t; Tuul and Bruno Morandi 11crb; MyLoupe 20clb; Paris Match Archive 15br; Sino Images 29cr; Paul Souders 42clb; Travelasia 43b, 61cr.

iStockphoto.com: aphotostory 12-3, 62b; bpperry 81tr; fotoVoyager 6cl; loonger 104t;

rabbit75_ist 25clb; VitalyEdush 18br;
willcao911 41tl; zhaojiankang 24-5.

Janes and Hooch: Ben McMillan 58t.

Jianghu Bar: 59br.

Mosto: 56t.

Mesh Restaurant: 59clb.

Robert Harding Picture Library: Directphoto
26-7.

Slow Boat Brewery: 59cla

SuperStock: Dirk Renckhoff / imageBROKER
47tl.

The Taco Bar: 93c.

Cover
Front and spine: **AWL Images:** Maurizio Rellini.

Back: **AWL Images:** Maurizio Rellini bc;
Dreamstime.com: Sean Pavone tr, Yulan tl;
iStockphoto.com: ispyfriend crb, Yestock cla.

Pull Out Map Cover
AWL Images: Maurizio Rellini.

All other images © Dorling Kindersley
For further information see:
www.dkimages.com

Penguin
Random
House

Printed and bound in Malaysia

First edition 2007

Published in Great Britain by
Dorling Kindersley Limited
80 Strand, London WC2R 0RL

Published in the United States by
DK US, 1450 Broadway, Suite 801
New York, NY 10018, USA

Copyright © 2007, 2019 Dorling
Kindersley Limited

A Penguin Random House Company

19 20 21 22 10 9 8 7 6 5 4 3 2 1

**Reprinted with revisions 2009, 2011,
2013, 2015, 2017, 2019**

A CIP catalog record is available
from the British Library.

A catalog record for this book is available
from the Library of Congress.

ISSN 1479-344X
ISBN 978 0 2413 6797 1

SPECIAL EDITIONS OF
DK TRAVEL GUIDES

DK Travel Guides can be purchased
in bulk quantities at discounted prices
for use in promotions or as premiums.
We also offer special editions and
personalized jackets, corporate
imprints, and excerpts from all our
books, tailored specifically to meet
your needs.

To find out more, please contact:

in the US
specialsales@dk.com
in the UK
travelguides@uk.dk.com
in Canada
specialmarkets@dk.com
in Australia
**penguincorporatesales@
penguinrandomhouse.com.au**

*As a guide to abbreviations in visitor information
blocks: **Adm** = admission charge; **D** = dinner;
L = lunch.*

Phrase Book

The Chinese language belongs to the Sino-Tibetan family of languages and uses characters which are ideographic – a symbol is used to represent an idea or an object. Mandarin Chinese, known as Putonghua in mainland China, is fairly straightforward as each character is monosyllabic. Traditionally, Chinese is written in vertical columns from top right to bottom left, however the Western style is widely used. There are several Romanization systems; the Pinyin system used here is the official system in mainland China. This phrase book gives the English word or phrase, followed by the Chinese script, then the Pinyin.

Guidelines
Pronounce vowels as in these English words:

a = as in "father"
e = as in "lurch"
i = as in "see"
o = as in "solid"
u = as in "pooh"
ü = as the French u or German ü (place your lips to say "oo" and try to say "ee")

Letter combinations
Most of the consonants are pronounced as in English. As a rough guide, pronounce the following consonants as in these English words:

c = as ts in "hats"
q = as ch in "cheat"
x = as sh in "sheet"
z = as ds in "heads"
zh = as j in "Joe"

Mandarin Chinese is a tonal language with four tones, represented in Pinyin by one of the following marks above each vowel – the symbol shows whether the tone is flat, rising, falling and rising, or falling. The Chinese characters do not convey this information: tones are learnt when the character is learnt. Teaching tones is beyond the scope of this small phrase book, but a language course book with a CD or app will help those who wish to take the language farther.

Dialects
There are many Chinese dialects in use. It is hard to guess exactly how many, but they can be roughly classified into one of seven large groups (Mandarin, Cantonese, Hakka, Hui, etc.), each group containing a large number of more minor dialects. Although all these dialects are quite different – Cantonese uses six tones instead of four – Mandarin or Putonghua is mainly based on the Beijing dialect, is the official language. Despite these differences all Chinese people are more or less able to use the same formal written language so they can understand each other's writing, if not each other's speech.

In an Emergency

Help!	请帮忙！	Qing bangmang
Stop!	停住！	Ting zhu
Call a doctor!	叫医生！	Jiao yisheng
Call an ambulance!	叫救护车！	Jiao jiuhuche
Call the police!	叫警察！	Jiao jiingcha
Fire!	火！	Huo
Where is the hospital/police station?	医院/警察分局在哪里?	Yiyuan/jingcha fenju zai nali?

Communication Essentials

Hello	你好	Nihao
Goodbye	再见	Zaijian
Yes/No	是 / 不是	Shi/Bushi
… not …	不是	bushi
I'm from…	我是 … 人	Wo shi ... ren
I understand	我明白	Wo mingbai
I don't know	我不知道	Wo bu zhidao
Thank you	谢谢你	Xiexie ni
Thank you very much	多谢	Duo xie
Thanks (casual)	谢谢	Xiexie
You're welcome	不用谢	Bu yong xie
No, thank you	不，谢谢你	Bu, xiexie ni
Please (offering)	请	Qing
Please (asking)	请问	Qing wen
I don't understand	我不明白	Wo Bu mingbai
Sorry/Excuse me!	抱歉 / 对不起	Baoqian/ Duibuqi
Could you help me please? (not emergency)	你能帮助我吗?	Ni neng bang zhu wo ma?

Useful Phrases

My name is ….	我叫 …	Wo jiao ...
Goodbye	再见	Zaijian
What is (this)?	（这）是什么?	(zhe) shi shenme?
Could I possibly have ...? (very polite)	能不能请你 给我 ...?	Neng buneng qing ni gei wo ...?
Is there … here?	这儿有 … 吗?	Zhe'r you ... ma?
Where can I get ...?	我在哪里可以 得到 ...?	Wo zai na li keyi de dao ...?
How much is it?	它要多少钱?	Ta yao duoshao qian?
What time is ...?	… 什么时间?	... shenme shijian?
Cheers! (toast)	干杯	Ganbei!
Where is the restroom/toilet?	卫生间 / 洗手间在哪里?	Weishengjian/ Xishoujian zai nali?

Signs

open	开	kai
closed	关	guan
entrance	入口	renkou
exit	出口	chukou
danger	危险	weixian
emergency exit	安全门	anquanmen
information	信息	xinxi
restroom	卫生间 /	Weishengjian/
toilet	洗手间	Xishoujian
men	男士	nanshi
women	女士	nüshi

Money

bank	银行	yinhang
cash	现金	xianjin
credit card	信用卡	xinyongka
currency exchange office	外汇兑换处	waihui duihuanchu
dollars	美元	meiyuan
pounds	英镑	yingbang
yuan	元	yuan

Keeping in Touch

Where is a telephone?	电话在哪里?	Dianhua zai nali?
May I use your phone?	我可以用你的电话吗?	Wo keyi yong nide dianhua ma?
cell phone	手机	shouji
sim card	卡	sim ka
Hello, this is …	你好，我是…	Nihao, wo shi…
airmail	航空	hangkong
email	电子邮件	dianzi youjian
fax	传真	chuanzhen
Internet	互联网	hulianwang
postcard	明信片	mingxinpian
post office	邮局	youju
stamp	邮票	youpiao
telephone card	电话卡	dianhua ka

Shopping

Where can I buy …?	我可以在哪里买到…?	Wo keyi zai nali maidao …?
How much does this cost?	这要多少钱?	Zhe yao duo- shao qian?
Too expensive!	太贵了!	Tai gui le!
Do you have …?	你有…吗?	Ni you … ma?
May I try this on?	我可以试穿吗?	Wo keyi shi chuan ma?
Please show me that.	请给我看看那个。	Qing gei wo kankan na ge.

Sightseeing

Where is …?	…在哪里?	… zai nali?
How do I get to …?	我怎么到…?	Wo zenme dao …?
Is it far?	远不远?	Yuan bu yuan?
bridge	桥	qiao
city	城市	chengshi
city center	市中心	shi zhongxin
gardens	花园	huayuan
mountain	山	shan
museum	博物馆	bowuguan
palace	宫殿	gongdian
park	公园	gongyuan
port	港口	gangkou
river	江，河	jiang, he
ruins	废墟	feixu
shopping area	购物区	gouwu qu
shrine	神殿	shendian
street	街	jie
temple	寺 / 庙	si/miao
town	镇	zhen
village	村	cun
zoo	动物园	dongwuyuan
north	北	bei
south	南	nan
east	东	dong
west	西	xi
left/right	左 / 右	zuo/you
straight ahead	一直向前	yizhi xiangqian

Getting Around

airport	机场	jichang
bicycle	自行车	zixingche
I want to rent a bicycle.	我想租一辆自行车。	Wo xiang zu yiliang zixingche.

ordinary bus	公共汽车	gonggong qiche
express bus	特快公共汽车	tekuai gong- gong qiche
minibus	面包车	mianbaoche
main bus station	公共汽车总站	gonggong qiche zong zhan
Which bus goes to …?	哪一路公共汽车到…去?	Nayilu gong- gong qiche dao … qu?
Please tell me where to get off.	请告诉我在哪里下车?	Qing gaosu wo zai nali xia che.
car	小汽车	xiaoqiche
ferry	渡船	duchuan
baggage room	行李室	xingli shi
one-way ticket	单程票	dancheng piao
return ticket	往返票	wangfan piao
taxi	出租车	chuzuche
ticket	票	piao
ticket office	售票处	shoupiao chu
timetable	时刻表	shikebiao

Accommodations

air-conditioning	空调	kongtiao
bath	洗澡	xizao
check out	退房	tui fang
deposit	定金	dingjin
double bed	双人床	shuangren chuang
hair dryer	吹风机	chuifeng ji
room	房间	fangjian
economy room	经济房	jingji fang
key	钥匙	yaoshi
front desk	前台	qiantai
single/ twin room	单人 / 双人房	danren/ shuangren fang
single beds	单人床	danren chuang
shower	淋浴	linyu
standard room	标准房间	biaozhun fangjian
deluxe suite	豪华套房	haohua taofang

Eating Out

May I see the menu?	请给我看看菜单。	Qing gei wo kankan caidan?
Is there a set menu?	有没有套餐?	You meiyou taocan?
I'd like ….	我想要…	Wo xiang yao...
May I have one of those?	请给我这个。	Qing gei wo zhege?
I am a vegetarian.	我是素食者。	Wo shi sushizhe.
Waiter/Waitress!	服务员!	Fuwuyuan!
May I have a fork/knife/ spoon	请给我一把叉 / 刀 / 汤匙。	Qing gei wo yiba cha/dao/ tangshi
May we have the check please.	请把帐单开给我们。	Qing ba zhangdan kaigei women.
breakfast	早餐	zaocan
buffet	自助餐	zizhucan
chopsticks	筷子	kuaizi
dinner	晚餐	wancan
to drink	喝	he

to eat	吃	chi
food	食品	shipin
full (stomach)	饱	bao
hot/cold	热 / 冷	re/leng e
hungry	饿	wucan
lunch	午餐	taocan
set menu	套餐	suan la
spicy	酸辣	la
hot (spicy)	辣	tian
sweet	甜	dan
mild	淡	xi can
Western food	西餐	canguan
restaurant	餐馆	fandian
restaurant (upscale)	饭店	

Food

apple	苹果	pingguo
bacon	咸肉	xianrou
bamboo shoots	笋	sun
beancurd	豆腐	doufu
bean sprouts	豆芽	dou ya
beans	豆	dou
beef	牛肉	niurou
bread	面包	mianbao
butter	黄油	huangyou
chicken	鸡	ji
crab	蟹	xie
duck	鸭	ya
eel	鳗	man
egg	蛋	dan
eggplant	茄子	qiezi
fermented soybean paste	酱	jiang
fish	鱼	yu
fried egg	炒蛋	chao dan
fried tofu	油豆腐	you doufuu
fruit	水果	shuiguo
ginger	姜	jiang
ice cream	冰淇淋	bingqilin
meat	肉	rou
melon	瓜	gua
noodles	面	mian
egg noodles	鸡蛋面	jidan mian
wheat flour noodles	面粉面	mianfen mian
rice flour noodles	米粉面	mifen mian
omelet	煎蛋饼	jiandanbing
onion	洋葱	yangcong
peach	桃子	taozi
pepper	胡椒粉，辣椒	hujiaofen, lajiao
pickles	泡菜	paocai
pork	猪肉	zhurou
potato	土豆	tudou
rice	米饭	mifan
rice crackers	爆米花饼	baomihua bing'gan
salad	色拉	sala
salmon	鲑鱼, 大马哈鱼	guiyu, damahayu

salt	盐	yan
scallion	韭葱	jiucong
seaweed	海带	haidai
shrimp	虾	xia
soup	汤	tang
soy sauce	酱油	jiangyou
squid	鱿鱼	youyu
steak	牛排	niupai
sugar	糖	tang
vegetables	蔬菜	shucai
yoghurt	酸奶	suannai

Drinks

beer	啤酒	pijiu
black tea	红茶	hong cha
coffee (hot)	（热）咖啡	(re) kafei
fruit juice	果汁	guo zhi
rice wine	米酒	mi jiu
green tea	绿茶	lü cha
iced coffee	冰咖啡	bing kafei
milk	牛奶	niunai
mineral water	矿泉水	kuang quanshui
orange juice	橙汁	cheng zhi
wine	葡萄酒	putaojiu

Numbers

0	零	ling
1	一	yi
2	二	er
3	三	san
4	四	si
5	五	wu
6	六	liu
7	七	qi
8	八	ba
9	九	jiu
10	十	shi
11	十一	shiyi
12	十二	shier
20	二十	ershi
21	二十一	ershi yi
22	二十二	ershi er
30	三十	sanshi
40	四十	sishi
100	一百	yi bai
101	一百零一	yi bai ling yi
200	二百	er bai

Time

Monday	星期一	xingqiyi
Tuesday	星期二	xingqi'er
Wednesday	星期三	xingqisan
Thursday	星期四	xingqisi
Friday	星期五	xingqiwu
Saturday	星期六	xingqiliu
Sunday	星期天	xingqitian
today	今天	jintian
yesterday	昨天	zuotian
tomorrow	明天	mingtian